The Angel
BOOK

Books by Charles and Frances Hunter

The Angel Book[†]
Born Again! What Do You Mean?
A Confession a Day Keeps the Devil Away
Don't Be Afraid of Fear[*]
The Fabulous Skinnie Minnie Recipe Book
Follow Me
God Is Fabulous!
God's Healing Promises[†]
God's Answer to Fat...LOØSE IT!
God's Big "IF"
Handbook for Healing, Revised and Updated[†]
Healing Is Yours
Healing through Humor
Hot Line to Heaven
How to Develop Your Faith[*]
How to Find God's Will
How to Heal the Sick[†]
How to Make the Word Come Alive
How to Make Your Marriage Exciting
How to Pick a Perfect Husband or Wife
How to Receive and Maintain a Healing
How to Receive and Minister the Baptism with the Holy Spirit[*]
Impossible Miracles
I Promise...Love, God[†]
Let This Mind Be in You[†]
Memorizing Made Easy[*]
Shout the Word, Stop the Thief!
Strength for Today
Supernatural Business
Supernatural Horizons
The Supernatural Spine
There Are Two Kinds of...[*]
The Two Sides of a Coin
Watch Out! The Devil Wants Your Mind
What's in a Name?[*]

[*]Indicates a mini-book.
[†]Indicates a book published by Whitaker House, New Kensington, PA 15068.

Available through: Happy Hunter Ministries

P.O. Box 5600
Kingwood, TX 77325-5600

website: www.cfhunter.org
e-mail: wec@cfhunter.org

The *Angel* BOOK

Charles ❤ Frances HUNTER

WHITAKER
HOUSE

THE ANGEL BOOK
Personal Encounters with God's Messengers

Charles and Frances Hunter
Happy Hunter Ministries

P.O. Box 5600
Kingwood, TX 77325-5600

website: www.cfhunter.org
e-mail: wec@cfhunter.org

ISBN: 978-0-88368-598-3
Printed in the United States of America
© 1999 by Charles and Frances Hunter

Whitaker House
1030 Hunt Valley Circle
New Kensington, PA 15068
www.whitakerhouse.com

Library of Congress Cataloging-in-Publication Data

Hunter, Charles, 1920–
The angel book : personal encounters with God's messengers / Charles and Frances Hunter.
p. cm.
Originally published: Kingwood, TX : Hunter Ministries, ©1999.
Summary: "Explains the different kinds of angels and their roles, as described in the Bible, and relates personal encounters with these messengers of God" —Provided by publisher.
ISBN 978-0-88368-598-3 (trade pbk. : alk. paper) 1. Angels—Christianity.
I. Hunter, Frances Gardner, 1916– II. Title.
BT966.3.H85 2007
235'.3—dc22   2007009970

2 3 4 5 6 7 8 9 10 11 12 ⦿ 14 13 12 11 10 09 08 07

Table of Contents

Hebrews
Jesus Christ Is God's Son

Long ago God spoke many times and in many ways to our ancestors through the prophets. But now in these final days, he has spoken to us through his Son. God promised everything to the Son as an inheritance, and through the Son he made the universe and everything in it. The Son reflects God's own glory; and everything about him represents God exactly. He sustains the universe by the mighty power of his command. After he died to cleanse us from the stain of sin, he sat down in the place of honor at the right hand of the majestic God of heaven.

Christ Is Greater Than The Angels

This shows that God's Son is far greater than the angels, just as the name God gave him is far greater than their names. For God never said to any angel what he said to Jesus: "You are my Son. Today I have become your Father."

And again God said, "I will be his Father, and he will be my Son."

And then, when he presented his honored Son to the world, God said, "Let all the angels of God worship him." God calls his angels "messengers swift as the wind, and servants made of flaming fire."

But to his Son he says, "Your throne, O God, endures forever and ever. Your royal power is expressed in righteousness. You love what is right and hate what is wrong. Therefore God, your God, has anointed you, pouring out the oil of joy on you more than on anyone else."

And, "Lord, in the beginning you laid the foundation of the earth, and the heavens are the work of your hands. Even they will perish, but you remain forever. They will wear out like old clothing. You will roll them up like an old coat. They will fade away like old clothing. But you are always the same; you will never grow old."

And God never said to an angel, as he did to his Son, "Sit in honor at my right hand until I humble your enemies, making them a footstool under your feet."

But angels are only servants. They are spirits sent from God to care for those who will receive salvation.

Hebrews 1:1-14 NLT

6

CHAPTER 1

My First Encounter With An Angel

By Frances

The study of angels is fascinating!

For most of my life, I never really gave any serious consideration to angels.

I thought about angels at Christmas time more than any other time of year, and if I happened to think about them, I probably would have thought about little blonde girls in a church play, draped in white sheets with chicken feathers pasted on their backs to imitate wings, wearing little crowns on their heads. That is the most consideration I had ever given angels...

...until I met one!

When I was saved, I was so interested in learning everything I could about God and Jesus that I didn't think about anything else. I didn't realize what an important role angels play throughout the Bible and what a surprisingly large part they would later play in my own life!

The first time I was aware of encountering an angel occurred in 1978 at the Civic Center in Abilene, Texas. It was a night I will never forget! The entire day had been extraordinary because during the morning worship service, the worship gradually, but noticeably, intensified. As we continued singing in an unusually high form of praise, there was such an electrifying anointing present that it encouraged us to go even higher in praise and worship. Everybody felt that anything could happen! No one wanted to stop praising God!

At some point during this incredible praise and worship, the pastor who was hosting the meeting glanced toward the top of the Civic Center. To his amazement he saw an entire row of angels positioned in front of the valance which hung all the way across the stage. He was so excited, he burst into an even higher realm of praise!

He looked up a second time, and was even more shocked because he saw another row of angels behind the first row. The second row was made up of much larger and obviously stronger angels! He asked, "God, I don't understand! What is the meaning of this?"

God answered him, "The first row are the *blessing angels* that I have sent to bless you because of the praise and worship. The second row are the *warrior angels* which I have sent to fight the spirit of religiosity in the city of Abilene, Texas."

Unfortunately, there is a deep-seated spirit of religiosity in every city in the United States and across the world. So many people go to their churches on Sunday morning and have two songs, listen to a prayer, give in the offering, "endure" a sermon and that's it. They go home and seldom think further about God until the next Sunday. They never think about Jesus through the week. Bound by a "form of religion," a spirit of religiosity prevents them from worshiping God in spirit and in truth and it keeps them from enjoying the fullness of knowing Jesus.

God said to the pastor in Abilene that He had sent this tremendous band of warrior angels to fight the spirit of religiosity! We were overwhelmed by this good news.

After the morning service had ended, the pastor shared with us what he had seen. Charles and I got so excited that we decided to look for angels! We had never seen an angel, so after seeing this pastor's exhilaration we got so wound up we thought we would just have to find some little angels in the auditorium. We looked under the chairs. We looked on top of the chairs. We looked in the choir section. We looked under the pulpit! We looked every place we could think of but we could not find a single, solitary angel!

We were so excited about what the pastor had shared with us that we asked him to share his experience in the evening service. At that time, we were unaware of the part angels play in our daily lives. God must have been dealing with us about angels to alert us and to send us to our Bibles to discover a lot more about these supernatural beings.

That evening, the pastor shared; everyone in the congregation was absolutely thrilled to learn about the "blessing angels" and the "warrior angels" he had seen. We could see by the expressions on their faces that they were planning to examine every nook and cranny of that building so they could see angels, too!

When the pastor completed his testimony, Charles began to speak on the subject of marriage. We each had a microphone, and since he was speaking, I began to move back slowly so the attention of the audience would be focused on Charles.

After I had retreated a few steps listening to Charles, a most unusual sensation came over me. The musicians had left the stage, and I knew there was no one there except Charles and Frances Hunter. Yet in my spirit I sensed there was another being on the stage to my left. I knew it wasn't God, and I knew it wasn't Jesus, but I also knew it was not a human being!

I was intrigued!

Not wishing to disturb the service, I continued backing up very, very slowly. As I inched back, I could feel the closeness of the being on the stage. I turned my eyes to the right side of the audience and very slowly scanned all the way across the audience, which I often do when Charles is talking, but I did not stop when I got to the left side of the Civic Center. I continued looking until I could see *what* it was or *who* it was standing beside me.

Then I got the shock of my life! Standing beside me was the tallest man I had ever seen! He was between seven and eight feet tall with huge, broad shoulders.

Instantly I knew it was an angel!

Totally enraptured by this encounter, my first with an angel, I forgot I was holding a microphone in my hand. I screamed, "WOW!" and that word resounded throughout the entire auditorium!

I had been so careful not to disturb the service but this certainly disrupted it! Unable to suppress my feelings of awe, I yelled, "WOW!" at the top of my voice. I wasn't afraid; the feeling I had was more of shock and amazement! Then God spoke to me in a beautiful loving way. God did not speak through the angel but spoke clearly to me through my mind and my spirit.

The awesome words He said to me are branded on my heart today, many years later, just as deeply as they were burned into me that night:

"That is a special warrior angel I have sent to protect you from the fiery darts of the devil until Jesus Christ comes back again."

Did you pick up the most special words in that message? He said, *"...until Jesus Christ comes back again."*

He did not say, "...until you die!"

He said, "...until Jesus Christ comes back again!"

There is no way I could ever express how completely full and overflowing I felt with the love of God at that moment. I was totally enveloped in His love, and filled with a love for Him greater than I had ever felt before. I was completely in awe of the fact that He had not only spoken to me, but that He had sent an angel to protect me! This was beyond anything my finite mind could even dream or understand! There was such an awareness of the awesomeness of God that to this day I do not remember the rest of the service. I know we continued it, but all I could actually think about was what I felt in my heart at that particular moment.

It was a time of thanksgiving, a time of thankfulness, a time of gratefulness, a time of appreciation that God would take time out to make that particular night such a blessing to me for the rest of my life!

The memory of this visitation and God's words to me have helped me through the many difficult challenges I have experienced since that extraordinary night!

In 1988 there was a terrible day when the doctors told me I had an incurable, fatal disease. They said that I would probably not live more than four to six days, and at the most I had six months, providing I spent those six months in the hospital, taking massive daily doses of antibiotics.

After hearing that horrible report, a death sentence from reputable doctors, I said, "God, You said for us to put You in remembrance of Your Word" (Isaiah 43:26). I reminded Him He had sent a special warrior angel to protect me from the fiery darts of the devil until Jesus Christ comes back again!

I put my hand over the mouthpiece of the telephone and said, "I don't receive that in the Name of Jesus!"

Immediately, all worry and concern disappeared from my heart. The peace of God which passes all understanding flooded my soul because long before, in 1978, I had received that beautiful personal word from God. God did heal me and I have never had any recurrence of that disease!

How Did You Know It Was An Angel?

Many times throughout the Scripture we find instances in which God sent angels to give consolation or comfort in times of distress.

A question that most people ask me when I share about my first encounter with the angel is, "How did you know it was an angel?"

I cannot explain how I knew except that I *knew*. I knew that I knew that I knew that I knew! When you see an angel, there will be absolutely no doubt whatsoever in your mind. If there is a doubt, the "angel" just might be a result of your dinner, or a product of your own desire to have an angelic visitation. When an angel comes to you from the awesome presence of God, though, there will be no doubt!

The next common question I hear is, "What does the angel look like?"

The angel God assigned to me is really BIG. He stands between seven and eight feet tall and looks as though he weighs about four hundred pounds. He has sandy colored, reddish blonde hair, perhaps a little more on the light red side than on the blonde side. His hair is curly, and believe it or not, he appears to be about twenty-five years of age. He looks old enough to be out of the teenage years, yet young enough to be strong, active and with the potential of being extremely powerful.

The night I first saw him, he was wearing a warrior's outfit, a form of mesh or chain mail. It was somewhere between a copper and gold color. The best way I can describe his appearance is to say that what he was wearing looked like what I might have expected a Roman soldier to wear. I knew instantly that when he was around, I didn't ever have anything to worry about!

Many people have asked me, "Does the angel have wings?"

No, this angel doesn't have wings! We see pictures everywhere of beautiful feminine angels with wings and of little cherub angels with wings. However, very few people that I have ever talked with who have seen angels have mentioned that the angels have wings. Although the Bible describes some of the angelic host, such as seraphim and cherubim, as having wings, in most cases the biblical appearances, as well as those recent manifestations we have experienced, involved angels appearing in the form of human beings.

Apparently angels can move with the speed of light, the speed of energy, or the speed of sound. Without the benefit of wings, they are able to go where they are directed much faster than if they were propelled with wings, faster than we could imagine.

Angels are eternal. They were not born but created. They do not age or die. God created them before the beginning as part of His eternal plan, and they are involved in His plan throughout the Bible. Angels don't marry, and they don't multiply. As a result the angels we encounter now have been around since the beginning of time! This is a fascinating thought! Since the angels were created before the beginning, they are old in years, but our angel, and all those I have heard about in other testimonies, appear to be young, strong and robust!

I am going to ask you to do something very special; as Scriptures are quoted in this book, read them out loud. I have discovered when I read Scriptures *out loud,* they become more of a reality. I believe you'll find that reading them out loud will do that for you.

An Angel Visits Zacharias

In Luke 1:11, the story is told about how Zacharias went into the temple at a very special time. Elizabeth, his wife, was barren and they were both advanced in years, but suddenly and unexpectedly the activity of angels began to create miracles in their lives.

> *Then an angel of the Lord appeared to him, standing on the right side of the altar of incense. And when Zacharias saw him, he was troubled, and fear fell upon him. But the angel said to him, "Do not be afraid, Zacharias, for your prayer is heard; and your wife Elizabeth will bear you a son, and you shall call his name John. And you will have great joy and gladness, and many will rejoice at his birth."*

This should have been wonderful and exciting news to Zacharias since both he and Elizabeth were elderly. However, instead of being excited, Zacharias was full of doubt as to the truth of what the angel said. One of the most important things to note in this story is the fact that it says *fear* fell on Zacharias.

Immediately the angel spoke to him, *"Do not be afraid, Zacharias."* There is such an intensity and such a presence of God with the appearance of a holy angel, that it can easily bring fear to your heart! The first words the angel said were precious, loving words of comfort to calm Zacharias' fears.

Fear can put a tremendous number of unholy things in your mind! The Living Bible says that Zacharias was not only startled, but also terrified at the appearance of an angel standing to the right of the altar of incense. When fear comes in, it opens the door for the devil to barrage your mind with thoughts that have never been there before! Doubt, unbelief, worry, skepticism, uncertainty, suspicion and distrust quickly rear their ugly heads at a time like this! This is what happened to Zacharias. He questioned the angel's statement about having a baby, and with good reason. At his age, babies are not the normal expected happenings in life.

The angel then said to him, "I am Gabriel, who stands in the presence of God, and was sent to speak to you and bring these glad tidings" (vs.19).

What a wonderful and exciting piece of information to realize that one of the chief angels, Gabriel, had been sent directly from the presence of God to speak to Zacharias. Can you imagine the glow on him? What an honor and what a privilege this was! God had sent a *special* angel to bring a *special* message to a *special* person at a *special* time.

God is doing the same thing today!

The angel promptly supported this with a statement that he would have joy and gladness and that many people would rejoice at the birth of their son because he told him that this son would be great in the sight of God. He also gave him a prophetic word, giving instructions that the baby must never drink wine nor strong drink and that he would be filled with the Holy Spirit even from his mother's womb. Gabriel went on to say that many of the children of Israel would turn to the Lord their God because of this miracle child.

"Zacharias was told before anyone else that God was setting in motion his own visit to earth. Zacharias and his wife, Elizabeth, were known for their personal holiness. They were well suited to doing a special work for God. But they shared the pain of not having children ~ long seen by Jews as proof of not having God's blessing. Zacharias and Elizabeth were old, and they had stopped even asking for children.

"This trip to the Temple in Jerusalem for Zacharias' turn at duty had included an unexpected blessing. Zacharias was chosen to be the priest who would enter the Holy of Holies to offer incense to God for the people. Suddenly, much to his surprise and terror, he found himself face to face with an angel. The angel's message was too good to be true! But Zacharias did not rejoice at the news of the coming Savior as much as he expressed doubts about his own ability to father the child the angel promised him. His age spoke more loudly than God's promise. As a result, God prevented Zacharias from speaking until the promise became reality.

"The record of the prayer in Luke 1 is our last glimpse of Zacharias. Like so many of God's most faithful servants, he passed quietly from the scene once his part was done. He becomes our hero for times when we doubt God yet are willing to obey. We gain hope from Zacharias that God can do great things through anyone who is available to him."*

Gabriel Visits Mary With An Announcement

Shortly after this event, there was a second appearance of Gabriel, and this is the visit which changed the future of the entire world, because it tells us about Gabriel's first visit to a young girl named Mary. Think about the supernatural environment at this particular time! Gabriel's conversation with the virgin Mary was very shocking because it says,

And having come in, the angel said to her, "Rejoice, highly favored one, the Lord is with you; blessed are you among women!"

Verse 29 reads,

But when she saw him, she was troubled at his saying, and considered what manner of greeting this was. And once again, the angel said, "Do not be afraid, Mary, for you have found favor with God" (Luke 1:28-33).

It was the angel Gabriel who brought the good news to Mary that she was to be the mother of Jesus. It is interesting to note that it was not a one-way conversation. They talked with each other because when the angel said she was going to have a baby, Mary said,

"How can this be since I do not know a man?,"

and in verse 35,

**Excerpt from the Life Application Bible*

The angel answered and said to her, "The Holy
Spirit will come upon you, and the power of the
Highest will overshadow you; therefore, also, that
Holy One who is to be born will be called the
Son of God."

Mary's response was absolutely incredible! She said,
"Let it be to me according to your word."
Another translation says,
"Whatever the Lord wants me to do, I will do it."

As soon as Mary had accepted the word from the
angel, it says, *"The angel departed from her."*

One of the exciting things about the appearance of
angels in the Bible is that they do whatever they are
supposed to do and they don't hang around. They get
on with their other work!

It is very interesting that in both of these appearances ~ the parents involved were told **before** they were
pregnant that they were going to have a baby.

Can you imagine how Mary felt at that particular
moment? She had just made the statement, *"Whatever
the Lord wants me to do, I will do it."* The angel left.
She was standing there alone, trying to accept the mag-
nitude of this word that had just been given to her by
Gabriel, the highest of all the angels in heaven!

I am sure there were many thoughts racing through
Mary's mind, the same thoughts that would run through
our minds today. Mary probably thought, "What am I
going to say to my mother? How am I going to explain

this to her? How am I going to explain this to Joseph? They will never understand." And yet, I am also sure that in her heart there was a divine calmness that was totally unexplainable because she realized it was the angel Gabriel who had brought this most unusual news to her!

Surely there went through her mind such thoughts as, "What am I going to do until the baby gets here, do I run off and hide so no one will know what has happened to me?" Many other thoughts along this same line must have come to her, exactly as they would come to a young girl today.

Think how blessed Mary was to have had such an incredible angelic encounter; imagine how blessed she was when she realized who this baby was whom the Holy Spirit was going to place in her womb. I am sure she did not treat this lightly, and even though many questions came into her mind, there must have been a tremendous joy in knowing that she had been chosen above all the other women in the earth.

One of the most important commitments God ever impressed on Charles was the expression, "Whatever the Lord wants me to do, I will do it." In 1968, from his heart, Charles said, "God and Christ Jesus, I am willing to do anything you **want** me to do. If I am doing anything you don't **want** me to do, tell me and I will never do it again. If I'm not doing anything you **want,** tell me. I would rather die than not obey your desires."

The Bible says in Hebrews 13:2,

Be not forgetful to entertain strangers; for thereby some have entertained angels unawares (KJV).

Most have the form of a human being and walk or talk just like an ordinary person. We need to be very sensitive to the fact that angels are among us all the time. Psalm 34:7 says,

The angel of the Lord [the angel that is from the Lord] encamps or lives around them that fear him, and he delivers us.

We have protecting angels who are encamped around us all the time! What a blessing!

In Hebrews 1:13-14, God shows us that He sent them forth into the earth to watch after us.

But to which of the angels has He ever said: "Sit at My right hand, till I make Your enemies Your footstool?" Are they not all ministering spirits sent forth to minister for those who will inherit salvation?

Angels have been sent to minister to us and on our behalf at all times. They are part of the multitude of blessings God has provided for us.

It may not be necessary, but we never get in our car without saying, "Father, thank You for Your traveling mercies. Thank You for the angels that surround us. Thank You for protecting us from those people out there, and those people from us, in the Name of Jesus." God may not need to hear this, but it is a comforting reminder to us.

Psalm 103:20 says,

Bless the Lord, you His angels, who excel in strength, who do His word.

God tells the angels to *bless* Him. If angels need to bless Him, then certainly we need to bless Him!

Another interesting fact is the statement that the angels excel in strength. We may get weak; we may get tired; we may get worn out; we may get sick; but they don't! When we ask God to send us an angel we know the angel is going to be strong and healthy, not sick and puny. He is going to be able to assist us in whatever areas we need help!

Before Jesus was born, there was tremendous angelic activity and we are totally convinced that the same thing is happening again today because of the imminent return of the Lord Jesus Christ!

CHAPTER 2

What Are Angels?

The word "angel" means "messenger" (from the Greek word "angelos").

Angels are mentioned in 34 of the 66 books in the Bible. Seventeen times in the Old Testament and seventeen in the New Testament. The word "angel" is used 108 times in the Old Testament, 165 times in the New Testament and 66 times in the book of Revelation!

It is also interesting to note that in the Bible there were 104 appearances of angels to men or women. John, in the book of Revelation, had more angelic visitations than anybody else (52) but a surprising thing is that in the book of Zechariah, the angel appeared seven times, but only five times to Daniel (and we remembered those visits), and four times to Elijah.*

Although the Bible mentions angels many times throughout the Old and New Testaments, only four angels are named.

*Information taken from Dakes Annotated Reference Bible, Copyright 1963 by Finis Jennings Dake and the New Testament portion copyright 1961.

Gabriel

And I heard a man's voice between the banks of the Ulai, who called, and said, "Gabriel, make this man understand the vision" (Daniel 8:16).

The name "Gabriel" is made up of two Hebrew words: *geber*, which means "valiant man" or "warrior" and *El*, which means "God." The name literally means "warrior of God" or "valiant man of God." This is very fitting since Gabriel is an archangel, the order of angels given exalted rank and power. The archangels are also used by God to carry out special assignments.

Michael

Yet Michael the archangel, in contending with the devil, when he disputed about the body of Moses, dared not bring against him a reviling accusation, but said, "The Lord rebuke you!" (Jude 9).

"But the prince of the kingdom of Persia withstood me twenty-one days; and behold, Michael, one of the chief princes, came to help me, for I had been left alone there with the kings of Persia" (Daniel 10:13).

The name Michael is a combination of Hebrew words which means, "Who is like God?" Michael is an archangel like Gabriel, but Michael is also named as "one of the chief princes." His role could be compared to that of a military leader, one who leads God's angelic host against the forces of Satan.

Abaddon or Apollyan

And they had as king over them the angel of the bottomless pit, whose name in Hebrew is Abaddon, but in Greek he has the name Apollyon (Revelation 9:11).

"Abaddon" means "destroying angel" and "Apollyan" means "destroyer." This verse is the only time this name is mentioned in the Bible and it refers to the "angel of the bottomless pit."

Lucifer

"How you are fallen from heaven, O Lucifer, son of the morning! How you are cut down to the ground, you who weakened the nations!" (Isaiah 14:12).

It's strange to think that when we hear the word "Cherub" we think of Cupid or picture fat little babies with wings, but did you know that Lucifer was a cherub? Cherubim is the order of angelic beings which direct and express worship toward God. Only the Cherubim are given the task of protecting the glory and holiness of God and proclaiming His grace. Before his rebellion, Lucifer was the most exalted and powerful of all the angels and was entrusted with the awesome tasks of directing the worship of God and protecting His holiness and glory. No wonder the betrayal was so great when the devil decided that he wanted God's glory for himself!

In addition to archangels and cherubim, the third order of angels is called "seraphim." The word "seraphim" comes from the Hebrew term "sâraph" which means "on fire." This is the type of angel that came to Isaiah with a live coal and touched it to his mouth.

Did You Know Angels Can Cook?

Then as he lay and slept under a broom tree, suddenly an angel touched him, and said to him, "Arise and eat." Then he looked, and there by his head was a cake baked on coals, and a jar of water. So he ate and drank, and lay down again. And the angel of the Lord came back the second time, and touched him, and said, "Arise and eat, because the journey is too great for you" (I Kings 19:5-7).

Angels Have Food And Eat

Men ate angels' food; He sent them food to the full (Psalm 78:25).

But he insisted strongly; so they turned in to him and entered his house. Then he made them a feast, and baked unleavened bread, and they ate (Genesis 19:3).

Angels Take Orders And Give Protection

If you make the Lord your refuge, if you make the Most High your shelter, no evil will conquer you; no plague will come near your dwelling. For

He orders His angels to protect you wherever you go. They will hold you with their hands to keep you from striking your foot on a stone. You will trample down lions and poisonous snakes; you will crush fierce lions and serpents under your feet! The Lord says, "I will rescue those who love me. I will protect those who trust in my name. When they call on me, I will answer; I will be with them in trouble. I will rescue them and honor them. I will satisfy them with a long life and give them my salvation." (Psalm 91:9-16 NLT).

We can see that God uses angels to accomplish many different and remarkable jobs!

Angels Have Ability To Speak Languages
Though I speak with the tongues of men and of angels, but have not love, I have become as sounding brass or a clanging cymbal (I Cor. 13:1).

Angels Are Glorious
For whoever is ashamed of Me and My words, of him the Son of Man will be ashamed when He comes in His own glory, and in His Father's, and of the holy angels (Luke 9:26).

Angels Are Immortal
But those who are counted worthy to attain that age, and the resurrection from the dead, neither marry nor are given in marriage; nor can they die

anymore, for they are equal to the angels and are sons of God, being sons of the resurrection (Luke 20:35-36).

Angels Are Powerful And Mighty

...and to give you who are troubled rest with us when the Lord Jesus is revealed from heaven with His mighty angels, in flaming fire taking vengeance on those who do not know God, and on those who do not obey the gospel of our Lord Jesus Christ (II Thessalonians 1:7-8).

After these things I saw another angel coming down from heaven, having great authority, and the earth was illuminated with his glory (Rev. 18:1).

Then the angel of the Lord went out, and killed in the camp of the Assyrians one hundred and eighty-five thousand; and when people arose early in the morning, there were the corpses ~ all dead (Isaiah 37:36).

Angels Need No Rest

And the four living creatures, each having six wings, were full of eyes around and within. And they do not rest day or night, saying: "Holy, holy, holy, Lord God Almighty, Who was and is and is to come!" (Revelation 4:8).

Angels Can Appear Visibly

And she saw two angels in white sitting, one at the head and the other at the feet, where the body of Jesus had lain (John 20:12).

Do not forget to entertain strangers, for by so doing some have unwittingly entertained angels (Hebrews 13:2).

Angels Operate In The Material Realms

But the Angel of the Lord called to him from heaven and said, "Abraham, Abraham!" And he said, "Here I am" (Genesis 22:11).

Angels Travel At Inconceivable Speeds

And I looked, and I heard an angel flying through the midst of heaven, saying with a loud voice, "Woe, woe, woe to the inhabitants of the earth, because of the remaining blasts of the trumpet of the three angels who are about to sound!" Then the fifth angel sounded: And I saw a star fallen from heaven to the earth. And to him was given the key to the bottomless pit. (Rev. 8:13; 9:1). Also read the entire book of Ezekiel.

Angels travel at an inconceivable speed. They move at the speed of light but they can be here and they can be there without even missing one second of time. We move in the natural material realm, and they move in the spirit realm.

Charles had to go out of town to see his mother one time and he said, "How can the angel be with both of us." But then he said, "It doesn't really make any difference because if you need the angel, the angel is with you. If I need the angel, the angel is with me." Isn't that an exciting thought?

Angels Wear Clothes

And she saw two angels in white... (John 20:12).

The work of angels is varied and wide. They are constantly at work in the spiritual and physical realm, even though we might not always see them. Here are some other interesting things angels do:

Angels Drive Spirit Horses

Now Elisha saw it, and he cried out, "My father, my father, the chariot of Israel and its horsemen!" So he saw him no more. And he took hold of his own clothes and tore them into two pieces (II Kings 2:12).

So he said, "Go and see where he is, that I may send and get him." And it was told him, saying, "Surely he is in Dothan." Therefore he sent horses and chariots and a great army there, and they came by night and surrounded the city. And when the servant of the man of God arose early and went out, there was an army, surrounding the city with horses and chariots. And his servant said to him, "Alas,

*my master! What shall we do?" So he answered,
"Do not fear, for those who are with us are more
than those who are with them." And Elisha prayed,
and said, "Lord, I pray, open his eyes that he may
see." Then the Lord opened the eyes of the young
man, and he saw. And behold, the mountain was
full of horses and chariots of fire all around Elisha*
(II Kings 6:13-17).

Angels Guard Gates

*Also she had a great and high wall with twelve
gates, and twelve angels at the gates, and names
written on them, which are the names of the twelve
tribes of the children of Israel* (Rev. 21:12).

Angels Wage War In Actual Combat

*And war broke out in heaven: Michael and his an-
gels fought against the dragon; and the dragon and
his angels fought, but they did not prevail, nor was
a place found for them in heaven any longer. So the
great dragon was cast out, that serpent of old, called
the Devil and Satan, who deceives the whole world;
he was cast to the earth, and his angels were cast out
with him* (Rev. 12:7-9).

*...and to give you who are troubled rest with us
when the Lord Jesus is revealed from heaven with
His mighty angels, in flaming fire taking vengeance
on those who do not know God, and on those*

who do not obey the gospel of our Lord Jesus Christ. These shall be punished with everlasting destruction from the presence of the Lord and from the glory of His power (II Thess. 1:7-10).

Angels Execute Judgments

Then the Lord sent an angel who cut down every mighty man of valor, leader, and captain in the camp of the king of Assyria. So he returned shamefaced to his own land. And when he had gone into the temple of his god, some of his own offspring struck him down with the sword there (II Chron. 32:21).

He cast on them the fierceness of His anger, wrath, indignation, and trouble, by sending angels of destruction among them (Psalm 78:49).

The Son of Man will send out His angels, and they will gather out of His kingdom all things that offend, and those who practice lawlessness, and will cast them into the furnace of fire. There will be wailing and gnashing of teeth (Matt. 13:41-42).

Then immediately an angel of the Lord struck him, because he did not give glory to God. And he was eaten by worms and died (Acts 12:23).

Angels Minister To Saints

My God sent His angel and shut the lions' mouths, so that they have not hurt me, because I was found innocent before Him; and also, O king, I have done no wrong before you (Daniel 6:22).

Then the devil left Him, and behold, angels came and ministered to Him (Matthew 4:11).

Are they not all ministering spirits sent forth to minister for those who will inherit salvation? (Heb. 1:14).

God's Angels Win

But the prince of the kingdom of Persia withstood me twenty-one days; and behold, Michael, one of the chief princes, came to help me, for I had been left alone there with the kings of Persia (Daniel 10:13).

At that time Michael shall stand up, the great prince who stands watch over the sons of your people; and there shall be a time of trouble, such as never was since there was a nation, even to that time. And at that time your people shall be delivered, every one who is found written in the book (Daniel 12:1).

Angels Strengthen In Trials

Then the devil left Him, and behold, angels came and ministered to Him (Matthew 4:11).

Then an angel appeared to Him from heaven, strengthening Him (Luke 22:43).

Angels Lead Sinners To Gospel Workers

About the ninth hour of the day he saw clearly in a vision an angel of God coming in and saying to him, "Cornelius!" And when he observed him, he was afraid, and said, "What is it, Lord?" So he said to him, "Your prayers and your alms have come up for a memorial before God. Now send men to Joppa, and send for Simon whose sur-name is Peter" (Acts 10:3-4).

Angels Direct Preachers

Now an angel of the Lord spoke to Philip, say-ing, "Arise and go toward the south along the road which goes down from Jerusalem to Gaza." This is desert. So he arose and went. And be-hold, a man of Ethiopia, a eunuch of great au-thority under Candace the queen of the Ethiopi-ans, who had charge of all her treasury, and had come to Jerusalem to worship, was returning. And sitting in his chariot, he was reading Isaiah the prophet. Then the Spirit said to Philip, "Go near and overtake this chariot." So Philip ran to him, and heard him reading the prophet Isaiah, and said, "Do you understand what you are reading?" And he said, "How can I, unless someone guides me?" And he asked Philip to come up and sit with him (Acts 8:26-31).

*For there stood by me this night an angel of the
God to whom I belong and whom I serve, saying, "Do not be afraid, Paul; you must be brought
before Caesar; and indeed God has granted you
all those who sail with you"* (Acts 27:23-24).

Angels Appear In Dreams

*But while he thought about these things, behold,
an angel of the Lord appeared to him in a dream,
saying, "Joseph, son of David, do not be afraid to
take to you Mary your wife, for that which is conceived in her is of the Holy Spirit"* (Matthew 1:20).

Angels Protect The Believers

*The angel of the Lord encamps all around those
who fear Him, and delivers them* (Psalm 34:7).

*For He shall give His angels charge over you, to
keep you in all your ways...* (Psalm 91:11).

*Now behold, an angel of the Lord stood by him,
and a light shone in the prison; and he struck
Peter on the side and raised him up, saying, "Arise
quickly!" And his chains fell off his hands. Then
the angel said to him, "Gird yourself and tie on
your sandals"; and so he did. And he said to
him, "Put on your garment and follow me." So
he went out and followed him, and did not know
that what was done by the angel was real, but*

thought he was seeing a vision. When they were past the first and the second guard posts, they came to the iron gate that leads to the city, which opened to them of its own accord; and they went out and went down one street, and immediately the angel departed from him (Acts 12:7-10).

Angels Impart God's Will

But at night an angel of the Lord opened the prison doors and brought them out, and said, "Go, stand in the temple and speak to the people all the words of this life" (Acts 5:19-20).

Angels Bring Answers To Prayers

...yes, while I was speaking in prayer, the man Gabriel, whom I had seen in the vision at the beginning, being caused to fly swiftly, reached me about the time of the evening offering. And he informed me, and talked with me, and said, "O Daniel, I have now come forth to give you skill to understand. At the beginning of your sup-plication the command went out, and I have come to tell you, for you are greatly beloved; therefore consider the matter, and understand the vision..." (Daniel 9:21-23).

Then he said to me, "Do not fear, Daniel, for from that first day that you set your heart to un-derstand, and to humble yourself before your

God, your words were heard; and I have come because of your words" (Daniel 10:12).

We know that God is the One to whom we pray and the One who answers our prayers. He is our source of strength in trials. God is the One Who takes care of us and meets our needs. But He can send the answer to our prayers via an angel. God can give us His strength through His messengers, the angels, and God can send His supernatural provision to us in the hands of His angels!

CHAPTER 3

Around The World With Angels

By Frances

Thus he became far greater than the angels, as proved by the fact that his name "Son of God," which was passed on to him from his Father, is far greater than the names and titles of the angels. For God never said to any angel, "You are my Son, and today I have given you the honor that goes with that name." But God said it about Jesus. Another time he said, "I am his Father and he is my Son." And still another time ~ when his firstborn Son came to earth ~ God said, "Let all the angels of God worship him" (Hebrews 1:4-6 TLB).

Angels were created to worship God and to worship Jesus. This is one of their primary functions!

Anointed worship and praise directed to God will often bring the presence of angels into a meeting. Several times this has happened in services we were conducting, or in services we have attended. When God sends His angels into your presence, look for the supernatural to happen!

While at a church in California I was privileged to experience some of the most awesome praise and worship I have ever felt or participated in during my entire life. I use the word "felt" because the presence of God was so strong you could literally feel it. There are many times when praise and worship is wonderful, but it does not always have that special anointing, or that supernatural power with it that makes you actually physically *feel* the presence of God.

This particular church is pastored by an ex-Mafia member whose beautiful Spirit-filled wife leads in the glorious praise and worship. One of the reasons for the incredible praise is that they require their praise and worship team to have a total and complete commitment to God in their lives. Praise and worship in this church often lasts for a long time but it seems to be for just a moment because the Holy Spirit-charged atmosphere so engulfs you that you are not aware of the passing of time.

At this particular service, I was praising and worshiping God with my eyes closed. Although there are a lot of people who worship with their eyes open, if I praise and worship God with my eyes closed, to me it is possible to block out everything else and really become absorbed in the presence of God!

During this very intense praise and worship, I opened my eyes for a brief moment. The entire front of the theater-style auditorium was filled with worshiping angels. It seemed as if there was an army of praising and worshiping angels standing there ready to block any activity of the devil!

The rest of the church had a cloud of glory floating over and permeating it. The cloud appeared to be a silvery gossamer fabric similar to, but thinner than chiffon. It was floating over and covering the entire church. Then it seemed to nestle down and cover everybody in the entire audience including me.

As we continued praising and worshiping, the presence of God became stronger and stronger. Energized by the presence of angels, I could actually feel a pressure on the outside of my body. It seemed as if God was literally squeezing my spirit out of my body because I felt His presence and His power so vividly.

Because I was sensing something in my spirit that I had never felt before, I leaned over and said to Charles, "Because of the intense praise and worship you could really just leave this earth very quickly, couldn't you?" That was exactly the way I felt. The praise and worship was so powerful and so anointed that it was lifting us into heavenly realms more than I had ever experienced. In fact, I really felt as if we were not even still on the earth during the praise and worship!

The church continued in wholehearted worship and I continued to participate. There is a tremendous difference in being a spectator and participating, and as I continued, my entire spirit, soul and body were so in tune with this incredible praise and worship that a very unusual thing happened.

I do not know how long it was after I said to Charles that you could just leave this earth, that the pressure on my physical body became stronger and stronger until it was so great and powerful that my spirit could no longer be contained in my human body!

Suddenly two angels appeared, one on either side of me. The angels were larger than the worship angels but not nearly as large as warrior angels. One on each side, they picked me up from where I was sitting, and my spirit and soul zoomed right up through the ceiling, escorted by these heavenly messengers!

I distinctly remember exactly where we went through the ceiling of the building! There was no sensation of passing through the ceiling even though I could clearly see my body as it went through. Before I knew it, we were in the heavenlies! The sky was the most brilliant midnight blue I have ever seen, and stars were twinkling by the millions. The same beautiful glory-cloud of gossamer-like appearance seemed to cover the entire sky that night as well.

It was an incredible, never-to-be-forgotten journey! Immediately after taking off from the church, we were over the North Pole. Even though the speed at which we were traveling was immeasurable, I had no sensation of wind blowing in my face or my hair blowing; only a slight ripple in my chiffon dress and the outfits of the two angels escorting me.

When we arrived at a place which was apparently close to the North Pole, the angels allowed me to drop down and see a church that was praising and worshiping God. This was very interesting because the light from this church radiated out about a hundred miles or even further. It was a brilliant light shining in the dark night; and even from as far away as we were, this light was easy to see.

It was an experience almost impossible to describe because as we dropped down to get closer to this church, it was as though we actually went down through the ceiling ~ just as we had gone out of the ceiling of the first church ~ and we could see the people inside the building. They were praising and worshiping God with their hands raised. There was a tremendous glory in this church because of the inspirational praise and worship.

Our visit was very short, or at least it didn't seem to me that we remained for long, but it was ample time for me to really see that this was a church which understood the value of genuine praise and worship. In just a few seconds, or a few minutes ~ however long it was, because I had no idea of the passing of time ~ we went back through the ceiling of the church into the sky.

But the journey wasn't over! Traveling rapidly through the night, the angels suddenly dropped me down so I could see another church. It was necessary for us to come very close to earth to detect the tiny light coming out of this church, whereas the light from the first church had radiated for perhaps a hundred miles. From as high up as we had been in the sky, the brilliance of that body of believers had been visible because of their praise and worship.

After we had descended close enough to this church, we entered it in the same way we had the other one. We observed that the people here had their faces buried in songbooks and they were merely singing verse one, two and four. There is a huge difference between praising and worshiping God and merely singing words from a songbook.

We stayed for just a little while and then once again we took off. In a whirlwind of time before returning to California, we had gone all the way around the world! Wherever we paused to observe a local church body, the exact same thing was true. When we could see a brilliant light radiating forth, we knew this was a church where they were offering true praise and worship to God. When we had to search to see a faint little light, we could see this was a group of people just singing. Singing never goes into the heavenlies as praise and worship does.

My trip around the world was so exhilarating and exciting that I cannot think of enough adjectives to describe the sensation I felt as the angels transported me for this special on-site learning experience! Then, suddenly we were back in the little theater church and I returned to my body in a very interesting way. As we entered the auditorium in the same way and place we had left, I saw my body sitting there, and in a flash of time the angels took me over to my seat and squeezed me right back into my own body!

I have absolutely no idea how long I was gone. All I know is that everyone was still praising and worshiping when I came back in, and after I was settled back in my body the worship stopped.

I have learned that when you have a supernatural experience, if you do not share it immediately, the devil ~ who comes to steal, kill and destroy ~ will try to rob you of it.

Because of having been in the presence of these angels who have been in the presence of God, I was so drunk I could hardly stand up. I asked Charles if he would take me up to the man speaking at the microphone because I knew I had to share what God had done. Charles had no idea that I had been on a celestial trip because he had been sitting there the entire time praising and worshiping God with me and was totally unaware of the fact that I had temporarily left this earthly realm.

Charles took me up to the stage because I was totally incapable of standing up by myself, and I asked the man who was making announcements if I could have the microphone so I could share this adventure with the entire crowd. The audience was spellbound!

Immediately after that, it was time for Charles and me to minister, and I had to have someone help me up the steps. I was so full of the presence of God that I felt as if I was totally and completely inebriated, drunk on the Holy Spirit, so lest I topple over, I said to Charles, "Help me up to the pulpit," which was another two steps higher. I hurriedly exclaimed, "I have got to have something to hang on to!" I simply could not get my head together after such a supernatural out-of-this-body experience!

Charles started the meeting which he normally never does! I was hanging onto the pulpit with every ounce of strength I had when I finally looked back and saw a chair three or four feet behind me! I decided that I might possibly be able to make it that far! It seemed as though it took me an eternity to travel those few feet. I finally made it! After I stepped back and sat down in the chair; it was over an hour before I finally got my mind focused enough so that I could minister.

What happened as a result of this angelic visitation is fabulous!

Words of knowledge and healings spontaneously broke forth immediately after I shared this around-the-world experience. It was a night of complete glory! The pastor said he had never before seen such instant miracles as he saw that night!

No wonder ~ we had been invaded by angels!

I appreciate praise and worship more than ever before.

CHAPTER 4

Touched By Coals Of Fire

By Frances

Each meeting gets more and more exciting as God reveals Himself in different ways daily!

A certain Tuesday night was a night we will never forget! It all started as Charles and I read the daily confession for that day, "Thank You, Father, that angels are in charge of me. I am surrounded by angels at all times who minister to me and protect me, even from accidents. I am accompanied by angels, defended by them and preserved by them because You have ordered them to do so" (Ref. Psalm 91:11, from our devotional book, *"A Confession A Day Keeps The Devil Away"*).

We were sitting in a restaurant as I read this and as soon as I finished, God spoke to me in that precious way He speaks to our hearts just because He loves us so much. He said, "Tonight there will be a visitation of angels in the church!"

I almost fell off my chair!

As we can see from the previous chapters, there are many promptings that can bring an angel on the scene. A believer's commitment, obedience, praise and worship, earnest prayers and speaking God's Word are just some of the catalysts which can initiate angelic involvement. There are also times when God chooses sovereignly to release angels into a situation, whether it's just for one person or for the whole world.

There is an incident which occurred when we were ministering in a tremendously anointed service, which taught us that *there are things which will keep an angel who is all poised and ready to minister to us, from being released to do so.*

During our morning service we excitedly shared with the people at the meeting that God had spoken to me and had said there was going to be a visitation of angels that night. Now watch what happened!

The organist nearly came up off of her bench because she said, "Last night I felt the presence of an angel so strongly down on the front row that I prayed, 'Oh, God! Let me see an angel!' And God said, 'Not tonight, tomorrow night.'"

She really got excited when she heard that God had spoken to me and this, of course, served as a tremendous confirmation to me!

Then the pastor jumped up and said, "You know, I'm going to share something I have never shared in all my life. Sixty years ago I was converted and I heard angels singing. I told my father the next morning that I had heard angelic singing and my father said, 'Don't ever tell anybody that, they'll think you're crazy!'" This pastor had never shared his experience with anyone else. About six or seven nights before we came to the church, he was talking to God and he said, "Oh, God! I have never heard the angels sing since the day I was saved. Could I hear them sing again before I come to heaven?" And he said God let him hear the angels sing again that night ~ angels singing in that beautiful way that only angels can!

Isn't it really wonderful to know how much God loves us and really cares about us? Here was a man who for sixty years had kept a secret locked in his heart and now suddenly he was sharing that secret.

We all sensed in our spirits that something fantastic was going to happen that night. We could hardly wait to get back to church to see how God was going to move.

There was great anticipation at the start of the evening meeting with an awareness of the presence of God in an unusual way. Suddenly a prophecy came forth saying that fire would come down from heaven that very night. The excitement mounted!

You just don't sit down and say, "All right, God, send those angels. I'm going to wait until You do." No, we conducted the service just like we normally do. I won't say I was "on edge" but I will say I was a little more sensitive to the Spirit of God because I kept looking around and wondering, "When are the angels going to come? When are the angels going to come?"

We spoke that night on the subject of "Total Commitment to God and Holy Living" because in these last days those qualities are extremely important in our lives. Our lives must be set apart from the rest of the world and holy because we don't involve ourselves with the things of the world!

I waited and waited, and we talked and talked, and I began to wonder whether or not the angels were really going to make an appearance after all. **Where did the doubt come from? Satan, of course!** We made an invitation at the end of the service for the people who wanted to make a total commitment to God to come forward and as they were coming up ~ without any fanfare, without any advance warning, in came the first angel blowing a horn that looked like a trumpet! He had wings and was not nearly as large as the angel that watches over us. This apparently was the signal for the other angels to come and in the twinkling of an eye, there were angels all over the place!

The only angel that I saw with wings was the first angel with the trumpet. The rest just moved through space, took their positions and then stationed themselves over certain individuals.

It was very fascinating because each angel had a pair of tongs and in those tongs were live burning coals of fire.

In Isaiah 6:6,7, where Isaiah had a vision in which a seraphim, an angel with wings, flew over to him,

having in his hand a live coal which he had taken with the tongs from the altar. And he touched my mouth with it, and said: "Behold, this has touched your lips; your iniquity is taken away, and your sin purged."

After that cleansing and purification, Isaiah could answer God's call by responding,

"Here am I! Send me."

Not everyone in the service could see the angels, but I could, so I just followed God's instructions. I walked over and touched a young man where an angel was hovering. As soon as I touched him on the lips, the angel placed the coal of fire on his lips and then immediately departed. The young man fell under the power of God and instantly began to speak in tongues. He had just been converted and didn't know anything about the baptism with the Holy Spirit!

As I walked through the audience, directed by the Holy Spirit, it was so exciting to feel the presence of God. The holiness of the angels was also something awesome! As I would see an angel hovering over this one, and then another angel over another one, and then over another one, an interesting fact surfaced! The angels did not place the coal on the lips of all the people involved! They were just at attention over an individual. They didn't place coals on anybody's lips until I walked over and touched the person very lightly on the mouth. Not everyone got a coal. I didn't understand it. All I knew was that I was only to go to the people God showed me had an angel standing over them with a live coal.

I felt that God was anointing them to really take the message of the full gospel out and carry it to the world, but the funny thing is that many of the people whom I felt would receive the coal *did not receive a coal.* However, I only touched the lips of those as directed by the angels. Jesus said He only did what He saw they Father doing, and during this trial, I was walking carefully in His pattern.

Suddenly, the Spirit of the Lord led me to the pastor who was sitting on the platform. There was an angel there and as I touched the pastor on the lips, God said to me, *"The biggest coal is for him."* And as I related this to him he really got excited, and so did I.

Then I went over and touched the lips of the associate pastor and his wife and he fell under the power. While he was on the floor, he reached up to feel his lips. Later he told me that he felt like I had hit him right in the mouth with a two-by-four! He thought his mouth was bleeding because he felt such an impact of power!

Some of the angels left with the same coals they brought.

Then God gave to Charles a tremendous prophetic word. *"Some of these angels will visit you between two and three o'clock in the morning and some of you who did not receive coals will receive a message."*

After a prophetic utterance like that, everybody wanted to go home and jump into bed and get ready for the angels. I have wondered since then if more supernatural things happened in the night than actually happened at the meeting!

Just to show you that God had everything planned in advance, we were not scheduled to speak at this church the following night, but God had graciously given us an open night between engagements. The pastor pleaded with us to stay over; we had the night open and we were available, so we agreed and then we understood why God had given us that extra night.

No sooner had we gotten to the meeting the next night than a lady came running in with a sack that looked like groceries. She gave them to me and said, "Here, I don't ever want these again!" When she had asked God the night before why she and her husband didn't get a coal on their lips to give them a special anointing, the only thing God had said to her was, "Cigarettes." During the night the angel came to this lady and said, *"The coal is for you when you give the cigarettes to God."*

I looked in the sack and discovered she had brought nine unopened packages of cigarettes and laid them on the altar of God. It's a wonderful exchange, isn't it? They gave up an addiction for a coal of fire from the altar of God.

There was another woman who came that night who told me an interesting story after the meeting. The way God does these things is sometimes almost unbelievable. That night God led me to talk on a very interesting subject from Numbers chapter 12. Let me share this with you because I think this is something very vital that we all need to understand.

Then Miriam and Aaron spoke against Moses because of the Ethiopian woman whom he had married; for he had married an Ethiopian woman. Miriam and Aaron began gossiping because

Moses had entered into an interracial marriage.
And they said, Has the Lord indeed spoken only
through Moses? Has he not spoken through us
also? And the Lord heard it.

Of course He did, because He hears everything we
say! These are two people who were favored of God but
who decided they would like to criticize one of their
brothers. The Bible goes on to say,

(Now the man Moses was very humble, more
than all men who were on the face of the earth.)
Suddenly the Lord said to Moses, Aaron, and
Miriam, "Come out, you three, to the tabernacle
of meeting!" So the three came out.

I wonder what the three of them were thinking about
when they came. It says,

Then the Lord came down in the pillar of cloud
and stood in the door of the tabernacle, and called
Aaron and Miriam (not Moses). *And they both*
went forward.

They were probably expecting to get something really good from God but He said,

"Hear now My words: If there is a prophet among
you, I, the Lord, make myself known to him in a
vision, and I speak to him in a dream."

In other words He said, "If you are a prophet I'll
make Myself known to you in a vision and I'll speak to

you in a dream."

"Not so with My servant Moses; He is faithful in all My house.

"I speak with him face to face, even plainly, and not in dark sayings; and he sees the form of the Lord. Why then were you not afraid to speak against my servant Moses?"

So the anger of the Lord was aroused against them, and He departed.

That's what happens when you begin gossiping about people ~ God leaves.

And when the cloud departed from above the tabernacle, suddenly Miriam became leprous, as white as snow. Then Aaron turned toward Miriam, and there she was, a leper.

Because she gossiped, God let her become leprous, white as snow!

So Aaron said to Moses, "Oh, my lord! Please do not lay this sin on us, in which we have done foolishly and in which we have sinned.

"Please do not let her be as one dead, whose flesh is half consumed when he comes out of his mother's womb!"

And bless his heart, *So Moses cried out to the Lord, saying, "Please heal her, O God, I pray!"*

Then the Lord said to Moses, "If her father had but spit in her face, would she not be shamed

seven days? Let her be shut out of the camp seven
days, and after that she may be received again."
So Miriam was shut out of the camp seven days,
and the people did not journey on till Miriam
was brought in again (Numbers 12:1-15).

Everything had to be shut down and nothing could
be done until Miriam could be brought back into the
camp.

I had no reason to be sharing this story except that
God told me to. The penalty for gossiping is spiritual
leprosy! Beloved, in the Christian world today if we could
just remember that when we hear a juicy little tidbit of
gossip about some ministry or person, we shouldn't
repeat it! We should pray for them because when we are
hearing gossip, it's an indication that that particular
ministry or person needs prayer.

When the service was over, a woman came out to
me at the booktable and she said, "Do you know what?
Last night at two-thirty in the morning, God came into
my room and spoke one word. He spoke the word,
'Miriam.' I didn't understand." She understood as I
taught because she had been extremely envious of somebody in the church. She was probably guilty of talking
against them because God said the one word to her,
"Miriam."

Do you know what we do when anyone says that they
want to give us a little juicy gossip? We throw our hands up
in the air and say, "Leper, leper, we don't want to be a
leper!" It is amazing how fast this will stop gossip!

I want you to try that sometime when somebody starts to give you some juicy little gossip that they heard about somebody else. Throw your hands up in the air and say, "Leper, leper, I don't want to be a leper!"

There was another young man in that service who years before had stolen a diamond ring. He had been in a hospital for the criminally insane. The police arrested him, he swallowed the ring and they couldn't find it but he later retrieved it only to have it stolen from him. God woke him up at three o'clock in the morning and said, *"You might think you don't owe for that ring because it was stolen from you, but you still do."* Immediately the congregation generously took up an offering to allow him to make restitution!

There were people in that church who had an appointment with God that night, but who didn't receive the hot coal from the angel and didn't get to move out into their calling because something in their life was preventing it ~ cigarettes, gossip, or failure to make restitution for a wrong. These and many other things are weaknesses in the flesh which we are responsible to deal with before we can receive all the blessings God has for us.

We can do things to initiate angel participation in our lives, and we can hold onto bad habits and sins that will hinder or prevent angels from ministering to us. It's not that we have to be perfect, because all of us are still maturing every single day! However, our willingness and sincere efforts to correct things that are not pleasing to God will both catch His attention and make it easier to have the angels involved in our lives!

Hebrews 1:14 says,

Are they not all ministering spirits sent forth to minister for those who will inherit salvation?

According to God's Word, we have angels who are just waiting to minister to us.

Angels are sent to glorify God!

They are sent to exalt Jesus!

They are sent to carry out God's plan!

They are sent to follow His instructions in accordance with the Word of God!

God's angels are sent to be a blessing to us!

CHAPTER 5

Angels On The Scene

There are different types of angels with many different purposes and jobs. Some of them are assigned to help and assist you and me! The more we learn to realize the potential of angels and remember to thank God for sending special ministering spirits to us, the more they will be a blessing to us. We are absolutely certain that angels are with us and performing mighty acts on our behalf day and night, without our ever being aware of their presence. We need to understand what the angels do in the Bible, so we will know what we can expect and be prepared for and praise God and Jesus for!

You can probably think of a time, perhaps when you were a small child, and were protected from danger; or maybe a time when you were driving and nearly had a wreck but didn't. God probably sent an angel at that instant!

Shortly after we were married, our daughter Joan was driving us on the freeway and exited onto the feeder street. It was early morning and traffic was heavy and the feeder street crowded. To her horror and ours, she discovered she had no brakes.

We were about to plunge into a truck or other cars. A bad crash was inevitable. All three of us instantly screamed "Jesus!" We are not sure what happened, but a small hole opened, seemingly not large enough for our car to go through. We missed the truck and the brakeless car came to a halt at the red street light! We know at the spontaneous impulse of calling on Jesus, God surely used one or more of His angels to protect us.

We instantly praised and thanked God for another life-saving miracle of protection! Hallelujah!

Angels From Birth Until Death

The most glorious account of angels being present at birth is, of course, the night of Jesus' birth in that lowly stable in Bethlehem.

> *That night some shepherds were in the field out-*
> *side the village, guarding their flocks of sheep.*
> *Suddenly an angel appeared among them, and*
> *the landscape shone bright with the glory of the*
> *Lord* (Luke 2:8-13 TLB).

Don't you wish you could have been present and seen enough angels that it would absolutely light up the whole landscape with the glory of God? This was just *one* angel whose radiance lit up the whole countryside! Then the angel reassured the shepherds because they were terrified.

"Don't be afraid!," he said. "I bring you the most joyful news ever announced, and it is for everyone! The Savior ~ yes, the Messiah, the Lord has been born tonight in Bethlehem!" Suddenly, the angel was joined by a vast host of others ~ the armies of heaven ~ praising God:

The very armies of heaven came out that night. Luke wrote,

a vast host of others ~ the armies...

Can you imagine how many armies there are in God's angelic army? I have a feeling that we don't even know how to count on our greatest calculator the awesome number. I don't believe there is any number in the human mind that we could possibly imagine which would tell us how many angels there are in heaven.

One Scripture which refers to the countless number of angels is in Revelation 5:11.

Then I looked, and I heard the voice of many angels around the throne, the living creatures, and the elders; and the number of them was ten thousand times ten thousand, and thousands of thousands...

And then the Bible says,

"Glory to God in the highest heaven," they sang, "and peace on earth for all those pleasing him"
(Luke 2:14 TLB).

Hallelujah!

When the angels finished heralding the birth of Jesus and rejoicing, what did they do?

When this great army of angels had returned again to heaven, the shepherds said to each other, "Come on! Let's go to Bethlehem! Let's see this wonderful thing that has happened, which the Lord has told us about."

Then the shepherds, after they went to see Mary, *went back again to the fields and flocks, praising God for the visit of the angels, and because they had seen the child, just as the angel had told them* (Luke 2:20 TLB).

Angels are sent not only to be there when you are born but angels are sent to be there when you die.

In Luke 16:22 (TLB) we learn angels are charged with our safe arrival in heaven. The devil is going to be up there, I'm sure, to accuse us before we get in, but the angels are charged with our safe arrival in heaven. This is for all the saints. Luke wrote,

Finally the beggar died and was carried by the angels to be with Abraham in the place of the righteous dead. The rich man also died and was buried, (not ministered to by angels) *and his soul went into hell.*

Just as the angels are active at birth, they are also active when a saint dies. They were ordered to carry the beggar up into heaven.

God is accelerating the exciting work the angels are doing right now in the present century.

Commitment Brings Angels

I love reading about and being involved in the supernatural things of God! Whatever God does that is beyond the power of man excites me more than anything I know of, so I especially love to read the Bible stories about angels.

Some of the most tremendous angelic experiences of the Bible occur in the book of Daniel. In the third chapter, the three Hebrew boys, Shadrach, Meshach and Abednego, are ordered along with everyone else to fall down and worship a golden idol which had been set up by King Nebuchadnezzar. These young men had honored God all their lives and they were not about to worship any graven image or pay respect to any god other than the one true God!

Nebuchadnezzar, of course, was furious and screamed at them,

"Who is the god who will deliver you from my hands?" (Daniel 3:15).

In other words, "If that God you worship is so powerful and awesome, why don't you have Him get you out of the fiery furnace you're headed for?"

I love what they replied, which in essence was, "Our God is able to save us, and if He chooses to do that, it's great; but if He doesn't choose to save us, that's still great, because regardless, we're still going to serve Him."

That is what I call real commitment, total commitment to God. I wonder how many of us would have the courage to say, "God, I would rather burn in a fire than to deny you?"

In verse 21 the narration continues:

Then these men were bound in their coats, their trousers, their turbans, and their other garments, and were cast into the midst of the burning fiery furnace,

where the fire was so hot it burned up all the men who threw our three heroes into the furnace! But then the king and his counselors watched in amazement as they saw not three but **four** men walking around inside the fire!

In utter astonishment, Nebuchadnezzar called the Hebrew boys to come out of the fire, and then he and all his advisors examined them to see if they had any scorched clothes or singed hairs.

Even if you burn wood in a fireplace, you have a little smoky smell on you when you leave the house, but the king and his staff couldn't even smell any smoke on these three youths. So the king changed his mind! He made a loud declaration in verse 28.

"Blessed be the God of Shadrach, Meshach, and Abednego, who sent His Angel and delivered His servants who trusted in Him, and they have frustrated the king's word, and yielded their bodies, that they should not serve nor worship any god

except their own God!"

What a blessing to know that God cared enough about Shadrach, Meshach and Abednego that He sent a special angel into that fiery furnace to protect them from the heat. He was the first fire extinguisher ever invented! A huge angelic ice cube! That's all I could think about when I read that, how God sent an ice cube angel to keep the boys cool in the midst of all that fire!

Notice that angels are indestructible. Metal, fire or mountains are no obstacle to them. When our angel appears on airplanes, part of his body may be inside the plane, part through the metal, and part outside!

When we are flying in airplanes, although Charles doesn't see our "big" angel physically, he often tells me exactly where he is. He says it's like a magnetic field of energy, and he says he could touch the angel on his nose, ears or any other part of his body. When I physically see the angel, he is exactly where Charles tells me.

God sent so many angels throughout the book of Daniel that I find it one of the most exciting books to read in the whole Bible! Another incredible account of unshakable commitment to God is found in chapter six. Most of us learned in church how Daniel, who was highly favored by the king, got into a real predicament because of the jealousy of some of his co-workers. These guys grew to hate Daniel and decided to get rid of him. But the only thing they could find to use against him was the fact that he worshiped God and prayed regularly throughout the day to his God.

They got real sneaky and went to the king, saying,

"Let's make a law that whoever prays to anyone other than you will be thrown alive into a den of hungry lions."

This was extremely flattering to the king, so he fell for it and signed the law to make it effective. Daniel refused to acknowledge the new law, and kept right on worshiping God and praying openly throughout the day. He didn't run into a dark corner, or hide in the basement to pray. He went to his regular place, and his attitude was, "I've been serving God all my life and I'm not going to stop now!"

When Daniel was brought before the king for disobeying the law, Darius recognized what had happened, and was grief stricken. I love what this king said to Daniel, as he was being thrown into the lions den (Daniel 6:16):

"Your God, whom you serve continually, he will deliver you."

Isn't that incredible? Even this king, who was a heathen, felt in his heart that God would not fail Daniel.

The princes and conspirators rolled a huge stone over the pit, to be sure Daniel didn't climb out and run away while King Darius

went to his palace and spent the night fasting: and no musicians were brought before him. Also his sleep went from him. (In other words, he had insomnia). *Then the king arose very early in the morning and went in haste to the den of lions.*

What do you think the king expected to find? Would Daniel actually be able to greet him, or would he be chewed up into little pieces? Darius called out, the Bible says,

with a lamenting voice to Daniel

to see if Daniel was in any shape to answer. That means Darius didn't have much hope at all and was already weeping and mourning in his heart that Daniel was gone! But I love what verse 21 says!

Then Daniel said to the king, "O king, live forever."

I imagine that from beneath the stone, from way down in the pit, a hearty, robust voice broke through the silence and the shock probably nearly knocked Darius off his feet!

Daniel went on to brag on God a little bit:

"My God sent His angel and shut the lions' mouths, so that they have not hurt me, because I was found innocent before Him; and also, O king, I have done no wrong before you."

Daniel had reaped a miracle because of his unbending commitment!

Those Old Testament accounts are so vivid, you can really get involved and almost feel you are participating vicariously. But let me share an exciting New Testament example of how commitment brings angels on the scene. In Acts chapter five we read

...so that they brought the sick out into the streets and laid them on beds and couches, that at least the shadow of Peter passing by might fall on some of them.

Also a multitude gathered from the surrounding cities to Jerusalem, bringing sick people and those who were tormented by unclean spirits, and they were all healed.

This is where the devil shows his agitation at what the apostles were doing.

Then the high priest rose up, and all those who were with him (which is the sect of the Sadducees), and they were filled with indignation, and laid their hands on the apostles and put them in the common prison.

But at night an angel of the Lord opened the prison doors and brought them out, and said, "Go, stand in the temple and speak to the people all the words of this life."

And when they heard that, they entered the temple early in the morning and taught.

Wow! Can you imagine the surprise of the high priest and all the Sadducees when they got out of bed the next morning and saw Peter and the other apostles preaching again? They immediately rounded up the apostles and brought them in for a reminder, saying in effect, "Didn't we command you troublemakers to stop preaching in the Name of this Jesus and confusing everyone with all your doctrine?"

I just love what the apostles answered.

Then Peter and the other apostles answered and said: "We ought to obey God rather than men."

Because of their commitment, God had sent an angel to open the prison doors, to let them out of jail so they could get back to preaching as soon as possible!

When you honor God, He honors you!

Obedience Brings Angels On The Scene

Closely related to commitment is obedience. God always favors those who are obedient to do what He says, even when they don't understand His purpose. God usually doesn't give a lot of details when He gives instructions, He just waits to see what we are going to do about it.

In Genesis, God asked Abraham to leave his family, friends, and neighbors to go to a land unknown to him. Abraham had the rare quality of unquestioning obedience. God liked what He saw in Abraham, and He promised him a child whose offspring would be *as the stars of the heaven and as the sand which is on the seashore.* But Abraham and Sarah had to wait many years before the child of that promise was born.

Can you imagine how much Abraham and Sarah loved little Isaac? Talk about the "apple of their eye!" I imagine there was nothing in the whole world as precious as each and every minute that Abraham and Sarah spent with their miracle son!

But God made a request of Abraham in chapter 22. It was simply,

"Take now your son, your only son Isaac, whom you love, and go to the land of Moriah, and offer him there as a burnt offering on one of the mountains of which I shall tell you." (God probably didn't bother to even mention this request to Sarah because she might have put her foot down and said, "Absolutely not!" or would have hidden him away in a blanket and run away, perhaps back to their homeland.)

Abraham loved God, and also feared and respected Him, more than he did even his own son. And that kind of unwavering obedience brought an angel onto the scene, just at the split second he needed one! For, as Abraham had bound Isaac and laid him upon the altar, and had his hand lifted up with the knife that would kill him,

...the Angel of the Lord called to him from heaven and said, "Abraham, Abraham!" and he said, "Here I am."
And He said, "Do not lay your hand on the lad, or do anything to him; for now I know that you fear God, since you have not withheld your son, your only son, from Me."

God has always looked all over the earth to find someone who would obey Him, whose heart is perfect toward Him (II Corinthians 16:9). He doesn't want to push and persuade, coax and struggle with the people He chooses, and yet, He will extend as much love and patience as it requires just to get some people who will finally say "No" to their own desires and "Yes" to His plans. When God finds this kind of people, their obedience will bring angels right on the scene to help out at their time of need!

Praise and Worship Brings Angels

The incredible high praise and worship that I wrote about previously brought a whole row of blessing angels and then another row of warrior angels into the service that night in Abilene, Texas. There was another time when I believe the highest form of worship possible went forth to God, and it had earthshaking results! This is another one of those angel encounters which really turns me on!

Paul and Silas had been out there preaching right and left, and as always had results that really turned the world upside down.

Their preaching was really irritating the devil, and that means he reared up his ugly head and caused the town people to become enraged. However, when Paul cast the demon out of a young woman who had been making her masters rich through soothsaying, it was the last straw! Almost immediately Paul and Silas were dragged away, beaten with a cat o' nine tails, and thrown into jail.

Have you ever visited inside a jail? It is almost unbelievable how cramped, cold, damp and unpleasant even our modern jails are. But those jails in Paul's day were literally a mess! Covered with caked blood from the many stripes, Paul and Silas were thrown into the dark, foul-smelling chamber and their shredded bodies locked in chains.

I love what the Bible tells us.

But at midnight Paul and Silas were praying and singing hymns to God, and the prisoners were lis-tening to them. Suddenly there was a great earth-quake, so that the foundations of the prison were shaken; and immediately all the doors were opened and everyone's chains were loosed (Acts 16:25-26).

Look what praise and worship did!

Who do you think shook the prison doors until they opened? Who unlocked all the prisoners' chains? It had to be strong warrior angels sent from the Lord God Himself to minister to God's servants!

Praising God caused the angels to come and shake that prison off its foundation. Praising God resulted in the guard and his entire family getting saved that night! Praising God opened the doors so Paul and Silas could be back in town preaching again in the temple early the next morning. Hallelujah!

Prayer Brings Angels

Daniel must have been one of the most godly men ever to live. He certainly had a lot of encounters with angels! He was a devoted man of prayer which had got-ten him thrown into the lion's den! He was also a humble man. God had given him great spiritual insight, and abilities to interpret dreams and visions. Yet Daniel never claimed to have any special power, but always sought God in every situation which needed an interpretation or explanation. Someone would come running to him with a problem that needed immediate attention, and Daniel would respond, "I have to talk to God first."

Daniel 8:15-16 tells of a vision Daniel had which he didn't understand. He sought God. He simply went to his room to pray, and suddenly there stood before him one having the appearance of a man. Daniel then heard a voice say, *"Gabriel, make this man understand the vision."* The Bible says when the angel came near, Daniel fell on his face, and at first he couldn't even move but was as if in a deep sleep. Daniel had been slain in the Spirit as the glory of this mighty angelic messenger approached him. His physical body just couldn't handle it. The angel had to help him up, and then began to explain the very troubling vision which was a revelation of the last days.

There was another time though, that Daniel sought God, and sought Him, and continued to seek Him, and it seemed that absolutely nothing happened. This went on for three weeks, and Daniel, having had such good results with prayer in times past, surely began to wonder if the heavens had turned to brass or was God mad at him, or what in the world was going on!

Then one day Daniel was down by the river. Maybe he didn't stay in his room all the time to pray, but liked to take little walks and talk with God outdoors and suddenly he looked up and someone had joined him!

> *I lifted my eyes and looked, and behold, a certain*
> *man clothed in linen, whose waist was girded*
> *with gold of Uphaz! His body was like beryl, his*
> *face like the appearance of lightning, his eyes like*
> *torches of fire, his arms and his feet like bur-*
> *nished brass in color, and the sound of his words*
> *like the voice of a multitude* (Daniel 10:5-6).

Again Daniel fell on his face when he looked up and
saw this magnificent angel clothed in the glory of God.
He did the same thing you or I would! He fell flat on his
face again! And he couldn't get up!

The angel helped Daniel up and began to speak to
him in such a loving way that reveals the closeness God
felt with this man.

> *And he said to me, "O Daniel, man greatly be-*
> *loved, understand the words that I speak to you,*
> *and stand upright, for I have now been sent to*
> *you"* (Daniel 10:11-13).

He must have known Daniel's thoughts. Daniel had
been wondering what had taken him so long.

> *"Do not fear, Daniel, for from the first day you*
> *set your heart to understand, and to humble your-*
> *self before your God, your words were heard;*
> *and I have come because of your words. But the*
> *prince of the kingdom of Persia withstood me*
> *twenty-one days;"*

Then he explained how Michael, one of the chief princes, had come to help him break through the demonic activity in the heavenlies.

I love this account, because it says to me, "Just keep on hanging in there, because your answer is on the way! Don't quit! Don't even think about giving up!"

God's Word has power that's working right now, and whether you see it or not, remember the angel said, *"I have come because of your words."* Keep praying and speaking God's Word! Your miracle is on the way!

God doesn't respect time or circumstances or give more favor to one person than another. God sent an angel to Daniel, who had been tremendously committed to Him all his life; but He also sent an angel to Peter, who at the time was a new Christian, who had probably been a pretty rough and rowdy character in his fishing profession.

Look at how prayer brought angels on this scene.

About that time King Herod moved against some of the believers, and killed the apostle James, (John's brother). When Herod saw how much this pleased the Jewish leaders, he arrested Peter during the Passover celebration and imprisoned him, placing him under the guard of sixteen soldiers. Herod's intention was to deliver Peter to the Jews for execution after the Passover. But earnest prayer was going up to God from the Church for his safety all the time he was in prison (Acts 12:1-5 TLB).

Beloved, pray that people are praying for you. As a matter of fact, I'm going to ask every person who reads this book to spend one minute every day praying for Charles and Frances Hunter. I don't think we could ever maintain the tremendous schedule we do or accomplish the things we do for God if people were not praying for us!

The story continues.

The night before he was to be executed, he was asleep, double-chained between two soldiers with others standing guard before the prison gate, when suddenly there was a light in the cell and an angel of the Lord stood beside Peter!

The angel was coming directly from heaven and the glory of God was shining all about him. I love what the angel did because he was so informal he just whacked Peter on the side. Can't you just see him going "pow"?

Have you ever awakened your children that way? When my children were little I used to tap them on the upper part of their leg and say, "Come on, come on, come on! Let's get out of bed!" And that's probably what the angel did to Peter. Peter was supposed to be executed the next day, but he was sleeping so soundly that the angel had to slap him to awaken him. That's confidence in God!

Verse 7:

The angel slapped him on the side to awaken him and said, "Quick! Get up!" And the chains fell off his wrists!

When the angel spoke the words that he had been directed by God to say, notice that the chains fell off Peter's wrists.

Then the angel told him, "Get dressed and put on your shoes."

It is beautiful that even though God could have instantly had him dressed, He didn't. He let Peter do a little something. God intends for us to do a little something, too. He lets us do things on our own to see if we are as interested in ourselves as He is.

And the Bible says,

And he did. "Now put on your coat and follow me!" the angel ordered.

So Peter left the cell, following the angel. But all the time he thought it was a dream or vision, and didn't believe it was really happening. They passed the first and second cell blocks and came to the iron gate to the street, and this opened to them of its own accord!

Peter didn't open the door, the guard didn't open it, nobody opened it. The door just opened. The angel probably opened it without even touching it. Think how God by His Spirit or by angels, opens doors for us.

And it says,

So they passed through and walked along together for a block, and then the angel left him.

He simply vanished. *When the angel disappeared, Peter finally realized what had happened! "It's really true!" he said to himself. "The Lord has sent his angel and saved me from Herod and from what the Jews were hoping to do to me!"*

Isn't that just wonderful to think that if you had the same problem Peter had, getting locked up in jail for preaching God's Word, that God would say, "Angel, go down there and minister to that child of mine."

Speaking God's Word Brings Angels

Psalm 103:20 proclaims,

Bless the Lord, you His angels, who excel in strength, who do His word, heeding the voice of His word.

God is moved when His saints demonstrate commitment, obedience, praise and worship and dedication to prayer. He is willing and ready to speak a word and send angels to minister to and for the heirs of salvation when we ask Him.

We are also able to speak God's word. In Isaiah 43:26, God says to remind Him of His word, and later on in Isaiah 55:11 He promises that His word will not return to Him void but will accomplish what He pleases. When God speaks, angels will hearken to perform His word.

Always look to God for your help, but thank Him for the ministry of the angels through whom He works. We can ask God to send angels but we cannot command angels to do anything.

Be committed! Be obedient! Be prayerful! Praise God all the time! Speak His word all the time! I believe in these last days you and I are going to see more of the supernatural than ever before. We are going to see more and more activity of angels than ever before in history.

God's Love For Souls

The writer of the book of Hebrews wrote,

Are they not all ministering spirits sent forth to minister for those who will inherit salvation? (Hebrews 1:14).

There are messenger angels. There are warrior angels, and there are angels who minister to those who will inherit salvation. I think this is one of the most exciting functions of the angelic realm.

God's plan of salvation is written all through the Bible from Genesis to Revelation. We have already shared about the night Jesus was born, and the glory that shone all over the place because of the brightness of the angels who came to announce that event. But remember, angels were involved in the thread of salvation even before Mary conceived. An angel had visited Mary to tell her what was going to happen. An angel appeared to Joseph to tell him what was going to happen. Then, when it was time to leave Bethlehem so baby Jesus wouldn't be killed, an angel warned Joseph to leave quickly and go to Egypt. The conception and birth of the Savior received a lot of angelic attention!

One of the main purposes for angels is one of the most exciting of all. God is really interested in the salvation of every person on the face of the earth. Think about this in connection with your own family. The closer we draw to the end of time, the more and more we are going to be aware of the activity of angels. The more we are going to ask God to send angels to do specific things in our lives. God can and does send angels even when we don't ask.

Angels are directed by God, and His heart yearns for souls to come into a right relationship with Him. Angels can be directed by God to go out and encourage, or push, or pull, or shove, or whatever it may take, to get unsaved people to those who will lead them into salvation. An excellent case of this in the Bible concerns Philip, who had returned to Jerusalem and was preaching the gospel in many villages of Samaria. Now watch what happened in Acts 8:26-27.

> *Now an angel of the Lord spoke to Philip, saying, "Arise, and go toward the south along the road which goes down from Jerusalem to Gaza. This is desert."*

Philip listened. It might not have been convenient, or on his daily agenda, but he listened and he obeyed!

> *So he arose and went. And behold, a man of Ethiopia, a eunuch of great authority under Candace the queen of the Ethiopians, who had charge of all her treasury, and had come to Jerusalem to worship, was returning. And sitting in his chariot, he was reading Isaiah the prophet. Then*

*the Spirit said to Philip, "Go near and overtake
this chariot."*

Did you notice that, when he was sent, he was sent
by an angel; and yet when he got there, verse 29 says,

*The Spirit said to Philip, "Go near, and overtake
this chariot."*

Did you see how God moved on Philip when the
angel said what the Spirit said, "Go over there in the
desert on the way between Jerusalem and Gaza because
I've got something for you to do." He sent an angel to
Philip for the purpose of bringing the Ethiopian eunuch into salvation.

God is doing exactly the same thing today! We have
people walk up to us in miracle services who say, "I
don't know why I'm here, I have no idea why I'm standing here." We will say, "We know why you're here. You
need to be saved." God has sent angels out to bring
them to the people who will minister salvation to them!

Right now while you're reading this book, let's stop
for a moment. Charles and I are praying and want you
to join your faith with ours and ask God to send angels
out to bring your loved ones to the people who will
minister salvation to them.

*Father, in the Name of Jesus, we thank You that
You created angels. Thank You, Father, that You
created them for such exciting purposes.
Thank You that You sent an angel down to protect Shadrach, Meshach, and Abendego right in*

the middle of the fiery furnace. They didn't even get singed and they didn't even smell like smoke because the angel You sent protected them.

Oh, Father, how we thank You that You protected Daniel in the lions' den. Thank you that You sent Gabriel down to explain the vision to him so that things he didn't understand were revealed through the angel who brought a message directly from Your lips.

Father, we thank You for Philip, too. We thank You that he heard when an angel of the Lord spoke. We thank You that when the angel said, "Go near," he got over there and did what You wanted him to do, and that was to present the plan of salvation to the Ethiopian eunuch!

There are many of us who have unsaved loved ones in our family. Father, we ask You in the name of Jesus to loose the vast armies of heaven. We ask You to send angels out there to bring (name of your loved one) to a person, to a point, to a place where they will find the living Jesus, where they will find Jesus as their Savior and Lord. We thank You right now! Thank You for dispatching angels and for sending them out. We thank you that those angels can do miracles in the lives of our loved ones and we rejoice even now. Oh, Father, the next time we see one of our *family who is not saved, we are going to chuckle to ourselves and say, "You don't know it (name), but you've got angels all around you shoving you right toward that person who is going to lead you to salvation." Hallelujah! We ask this in the name of Jesus!*

Here is another example of how God sees a person's heart and will sovereignly initiate angelic intervention in order to bring them to salvation:

In the tenth chapter of Acts, Cornelius, an Italian Gentile, who was devoted to prayer and helping the poor, was really seeking to please the God he believed was out there somewhere, but he wasn't saved! So God sent an angel down to tell him there was a man he must talk with, the apostle Peter, who would show him the way of salvation. God knew Cornelius' heart had really been seeking salvation, and He made sure he would find it! As a result, Cornelius' heart was divinely prepared and he and his whole household were gloriously saved. He was the first of the Gentiles to receive the baptism with the Holy Spirit!

The mighty angels of God are everywhere. There are more than enough to go around. And they are anxious to do God's bidding! One of the ways we pray for the lost is to ask God to send someone with the good news of Jesus to each one whose heart would be willing to receive Him. We believe that there are angels working in every tribe and nation, preparing laborers to go and hearts to receive. In Psalm 2:8, God says,

"Ask of Me, and I will give you the nations for your inheritance."

I'm certain we would be absolutely amazed if we knew all that God was having angels do all over the world right at this instant, because of His love for souls.

God's Compassion

There are times when God will look upon someone in their circumstances with such love and compassion that He will "move heaven and earth" so to speak, just to let them know He's in control. It might be someone who has served Him faithfully, or it might be someone who belongs to someone who has served him faithfully.

One of the stories which I have always thought was very beautiful involved Abraham's first son ~ Ishmael, not Isaac. Ishmael was not the son God had promised Abraham and Sarah, which was a special covenant agreement, but was the offspring of a union between Abraham and Sarah's maid, Hagar. Nonetheless, Ishmael was Abraham's seed.

One day, because of strife in the household, Hagar and Ishmael had been cast out into the desert to fend for themselves.

The Bible says,

Therefore she said to Abraham, "Cast out this bondswoman and her son; for the son of this bondswoman shall not be heir with my son, namely with Isaac" (21:14).

*So Abraham rose early in the morning, and took
bread and a skin of water; and putting it on her
shoulder, he gave it and the boy to Hagar, and
sent her away! Then she departed and wandered
in the Wilderness of Beersheba.*

*And the water in the skin was used up, and she
placed the boy under one of the shrubs. She went
and sat down across from him at a distance of
about a bowshot; for she said to herself, "Let me
not see the death of the boy." So she sat opposite
him, and lifted her voice and wept.*

*And God heard the voice of the lad. Then the
angel of God called to Hagar out of heaven, and
said to her, "What ails you, Hagar? Fear not, for
God has heard the voice of the lad where he is.
Arise, lift up the lad and hold him with your
hand, for I will make him a great nation." And
God opened her eyes, and she saw a well of water. Then she went and filled the skin with water,
and gave the lad a drink* (Genesis 21:10-19).

God was moved with compassion because this was a
child of His friend Abraham, so He sent an angel messenger to encourage Hagar with a promise for the future
and provided the miracle of provision they needed right
at that moment.

Another account which really shows the compassion
of God is in Acts where Paul had been taken prisoner

and was on a ship bound for Rome. After putting out to sea, they had run into a tremendous storm which lasted day after day after day. The crew all feared for their lives because they knew the ship was going to break into tiny splinters before the storm passed.

Finally the ship ran aground, and began to break up. But, before everyone panicked, Paul said to them in Acts 27:22-24,

> *"And now I urge you to take heart, for there will be no loss of life among you, but only of the ship."*

What he was telling them was, "The ship is going down but cheer up and don't worry, nobody's going to lose their life!"

Paul could speak so positively because an angel had already been sent by God with a word of encouragement. He continued,

> *"For there stood by me this night an angel of the God to whom I belong and whom I serve, saying 'Do not be afraid, Paul; you must be brought before Caesar; and indeed God has granted you all those who sail with you!"*

God did not have any obligation to all those sailors to send an angel to cheer them up. His plan was to take care of Paul and get him to Rome. He could have just comforted Paul by the Holy Spirit, or made sure Paul got hold of a piece of wood to hang onto and test his faith. God's heart is one of compassion. Sometimes He will send an angel from the throne room to the earth just to encourage and bring peace to a faithful servant.

God is so interested in every single believer that not only will He use supernatural means to protect them, He will also send angelic messengers ~ seen or unseen ~ to comfort, strengthen or encourage His child during a time of crisis. In this situation, God also knew the sailors were scared, and He sent an angel to give Paul a word of encouragement not just for himself but for everyone traveling with him!

God's Judgment

Although I believe God's preference for angelic visitations is for blessing and ministering to His people, there have been throughout the Bible, and will be in days to come, instances where God used and will use the angels to enforce His judgment on wickedness.

Angels were involved in the destruction of Sodom and Gomorrah. God first sent an angel to warn Abraham's nephew Lot. Then angels hurried Lot and his wife and daughters out of the city, even grabbing their hands and yanking them along because they were poking along too slowly!

And while he lingered, the men (angels) took hold of his hand, his wife's hand, and the hands of his two daughters, the Lord being merciful to him, and they brought him out and set him outside the city (Genesis 19:16).

One of the angels warned the group not to look back, but Lot's wife disobeyed and remained on the edge of town as a statue of salt.

Angels can still be sent to warn us of impending danger, and ignoring them can be disastrous!

We need to be alert to realize the potential of angels and remember to thank God for sending special ministering spirits to us.

CHAPTER 6

Ministering Angels

Beloved, did you ever think just a little tiny bit about a subject in the Bible and then suddenly it came alive and you had a tremendous desire ~ an overwhelming feeling that you had to find out everything there was about it?

That is exactly what happened to us on the subject of angels. Two verses in Psalm became real to us and started this tremendous interest in angels.

Angels Watching Over You

He shall give His angels charge over you, to keep you in all your ways. They shall bear you up in their hands, lest you dash your foot against a stone.

The Living Bible states it eloquently.

How then can evil overtake me or any plague come near? For He orders His angels to protect you wherever you go. They will steady you with their hands to keep you from stumbling against

the rocks on the trails. You can safely meet a lion
or step on poisonous snakes, yes, even trample
them beneath your feet! (Psalm 91:11,12).

Growing Up In The Lord

We had such a tremendous time with and enjoyed
our little granddaughter Charity so much because Joan
and Bob, our daughter and son-in-law, have really raised
her in the fear and admonition of the Lord. When our
oldest granddaughter was only two years old, we would
say, "Charity, how are you?" She would answer, "I'm
blessed." It always delighted us to hear her give her little
confession. That's scriptural because all the blessings
that God gave to Abraham belong to you and to me!
Then she would say, "I have favor with God." All the
blessings and all the covenants that God made with
Abraham are the things that make us have favor with
God. But the third thing she said really fascinated me
because she said, "Angels have charge over me."

Do you know what prompted this? One Halloween
she was afraid because kids were running around saying, "Boo!" and jumping out from behind bushes dressed
like ghosts. When she came back into the house she
said to her mother, "Oooh, Mommie, I'm so scared!"
Her mother said, "You don't ever have to be afraid because God gives His angels charge over you. His angels
watch over you all the time, that's why you don't ever
have to be afraid of anything." Jesus referred to children
having angels when He said,

"Take heed that you do not despise one of these
little ones, for I say to you that in heaven their

angels always see the face of My Father who is in heaven (Matthew 18:10).

What a wonderful way to be brought up! How I wish I had brought my children up in exactly the same way.

We believe the activity of angels is accelerating today because the return of Jesus is imminent. We began an intensive study of angelic activity in the Bible and we began to hear more and more about the activity of angels at the present time.

There are many times when angels have been with all of us, but we have just not realized it. Perhaps because of too little teaching or too little expectancy, we have not recognized the tremendous amount of angelic activities all around us.

Many times we think it is the Holy Spirit, and I'm sure that the angels take instructions from the Holy Spirit, but nevertheless, I believe there are times when angels are sent out as spirit messengers from God. They are dispatched by and instructed by the Holy Spirit but the angels actually come to us to deliver a message from God.

An Angelic Message For Abraham And Sarah

The Bible makes some very interesting statements where it is talking about the birth or the anticipated birth of a son for Abraham and Sarah. Notice very carefully that the first time they were advised about having a baby it was apparently God speaking to them directly. (Genesis 15:1-6)

After these things the word of the Lord came to Abram in a vision, saying, "Do not be afraid, Abram. I am your shield, your exceedingly great reward."

But Abram said, "Lord God, what will You give me, seeing I go childless, and the heir of my house is Eliezer of Damascus?"

Then Abram said "Look, You have given me no offspring; indeed one born in my house is my heir!"

And behold, the word of the Lord came to him, saying, "This one shall not be your heir, but one who will come from your own body shall be your heir."

Descendants as numerous as the stars

*Then He brought him outside and said, "Look now toward heaven, and count the stars if you are able to number them." And He said to him, "So shall your descendants be." **And he believed in the Lord, and He accounted it to him for righteousness.***

The next time we hear about this is very interesting but notice the difference! (Genesis 17:1-4)

When Abram was ninety-nine years old, the Lord appeared to Abram and said to him, "I am Almighty God; walk before Me and be blameless.

And I will make My covenant between Me and
you, and will multiply you exceedingly."
Then Abram fell on his face, and God talked
with him, saying: "As for Me, behold, My cov-
enant is with you, and you shall be a father of
many nations.
No longer shall your name be called Abram, but
your name shall be Abraham; for I have made
you a father of many nations.
I will make you exceedingly fruitful; and I will make
nations of you, and kings shall come from you."

A little bit later, God spoke to Sarah. Up until that
time she was called Sarai but then God changed her
name to Sarah which means "Princess."

An Angelic Appearance

In the 18th chapter of Genesis notice that the Lord
appeared apparently in the form of a human being, along
with angels, or was it an angel that appeared? Look what
it says.

Then the Lord appeared to him by the terebinth
trees of Mamre, as he was sitting in the tent door
in the heat of the day.
So he lifted his eyes and looked, and behold,
three men were standing by him; and when he
saw them, he ran from the tent door to meet
them, and bowed himself to the ground, and said,
"My Lord, if I have now found favor in Your

sight, do not pass on by Your servant.
"Please let a little water be brought, and wash
your feet, and rest yourselves under the tree.

Abraham shows hospitality

"And I will bring a morsel of bread, that you
may refresh your hearts. After that you may pass
by, inasmuch as you have come to your servant."
And they said, "Do as you have said."
So Abraham hastened into the tent to Sarah and
said, "Quickly, make ready three measures of fine
meal; knead it and make cakes."
And Abraham ran to the herd, took a tender and
good calf, gave it to a young man, and he has-
tened to prepare it.
So he took butter and milk and the calf which he
had prepared, and set it before them; and he stood
by them under the tree as they ate.

Again God promises a son

Then they said to him, "Where is Sarah your
wife?" And he said, "Here, in the tent."
(note that the Lord was speaking through these
three people who were apparently angels.)

Have You Entertained Angels?

In another place, the Bible says,
"Be careful lest you entertain angels unaware." "I
will certainly return to you according to the time

of life, and behold, Sarah your wife shall have a son." And Sarah was listening in the tent door which was behind him.

Now Abraham and Sarah were old, well advanced in age; and Sarah had passed the age of childbearing.

Therefore Sarah laughed within herself saying, "After I have grown old, shall I have pleasure, my lord being old also?"

God knows everything we do and everything we say and everything we think!

And the Lord said to Abraham, "Why did Sarah laugh, saying, 'Shall I surely bear a child, since I am old?'

"Is anything too hard for the Lord? At the appointed time I will return to you, according to the time of life, and Sarah shall have a son."

In this instance God spoke directly to Abram for the first time. The second time it was angels who spoke the word of God through what appeared to be human beings. Whenever angels speak, it is always the word of God. Angels will never say anything that does not line up perfectly with the word of God because the angels are the spirit messengers sent out by the Almighty God.

The Bible doesn't specifically record whether the angels were with Jesus all the time, although I think that there are angels busy on our behalf at all times, if we only could realize and appreciate what they are doing for us. I have a feeling that many of us might be having a real bad time if we didn't have so many angels out there taking care of a lot of our battles for us, because one of the purposes of the angels is that God has given them charge over you to keep you in all your ways. In other words, to keep you healthy, or strong, or to keep you from danger. I have a feeling if you looked around right now you might discover yourself surrounded by angels wherever you are if you could see with your spirit eyes instead of your natural eyes!

Even though the Bible doesn't record whether the angels were with Jesus all the time, there are many instances given when they were.

An Angel Announces The Birth Of Jesus

In the life of Jesus, the angel was there to tell Mary about Him before He was ever conceived and then the angels were there again at His birth. Later an angel spoke to Joseph and told him to take Mary and the baby away because King Herod was going to issue an edict that all the babies were going to be killed. It was an angel who brought that message to Joseph to save Jesus' life!

It was an angel who appeared to Joseph in Egypt and told him to return home. Angels ministered to Jesus after He was tempted in the wilderness. They ministered to Him at Gethsemane and they were there when He rose from the grave. At the sound of the trumpet angels will gather His elect, and in the great end-of-time, grand finale, angels will return with the Son of man.

Angels were totally involved in the life of Jesus and He is our example. Angels are totally involved in the lives of believers.

After Jesus was baptized in water and the Holy Spirit came on him, descending like a dove and alighting upon Him, the voice from heaven said,

> *"This is **My** beloved Son, in whom I am well pleased"* (Matthew 3:17).

Now watch what follows in Matthew 4. Here comes the devil!

> *Then Jesus was led up by the Spirit into the wilderness to be tempted by the devil.*
>
> *And when He had fasted forty days and forty nights, afterward He was hungry.*
>
> *Now when the tempter came to Him, he said, "If You are the Son of God, command that these stones become bread."*
>
> *But He answered and said, "It is written, 'Man shall not live by bread alone, but by every word that proceeds from the mouth of God.'"*

The devil tempted Jesus in three different areas during this time. The first time, we see Jesus being tempted on the physical or fleshly level; He was hungry and the devil offered him food.

> *Then the devil took Him up into the holy city, set Him on a pinnacle of the temple,*
>
> *And said to Him, "If You are the Son of God,*

throw Yourself down. For it is written: 'He shall give his angels charge concerning you,' and, 'In their hands they shall bear you up, lest you dash your foot against a stone.'"
Jesus said to him, "It is written again, 'You shall not tempt the Lord your God.'"

In this instance, the devil tempts Jesus on the level of emotions or the level of the soul. Satan was trying to tempt Jesus into fear, which appears in our minds.

Again, the devil took Him up on an exceedingly high mountain, and showed Him all the kingdoms of the world and their glory.
And he said to Him, "All these things I will give You, if You will fall down and worship me."
Then Jesus said to him, "Away with you, Satan! For it is written, 'You shall worship the Lord your God, and Him only you shall serve.'"

Finally, the devil tempts Jesus on a spiritual level. Could he actually get Jesus to use His supernatural power for selfish reasons or selfish gain? Remember, the devil wanted to exalt himself above God, exactly what he was trying to get Jesus to do!

Then the devil left Him, and behold, angels came and ministered to Him (Matthew 4:1-11).

In all three temptations, we see Jesus overcame the devil by the Word of God and immediately thereafter "angels came and ministered to Him."

You and I know that testing will inevitably come to us if we are truly serving God. Many times, the temptations we encounter are beyond human logic. That's why we can never counter the devil with logic or reason, only by the Word of God. We can believe that, just as angels ministered to Jesus after this victory overy Satan, God will send angels to minister to us.

Angels In Times Of Sorrow, Grief And Danger

One of the purposes of angels is to minister to us in times of sorrow, to minister to us in times of grief, to minister to us in times of danger, to minister to us in times of sickness and for innumerable other reasons.

The Bible doesn't say exactly how the angels ministered to Jesus. Maybe they brought Him food, maybe they brought Him something to drink when this tempting was all over, but it does say that the angels ministered to Him. They could have even held his head in their lap and just let Him lie down for some much needed peace and sleep. Angels are sent upon direct command by God Himself, and everything God's angels do is good and perfect!

Whenever we get on an airplane, we always ask God to send His angels to hold the plane up. Many times we tell people on a plane who seem to be a little bit nervous or a little bit upset if there is a storm in the air, "Don't worry! God has His angels holding up the wings of this plane, so you don't have to worry about it."

That is exactly the way I feel. I feel that God's angels can do so much if we will remember to say, "God, would you send your angels along?"

God oftentimes gives through an angel the greatest messages He has to give and the most outstanding information He wants to relate.

We need to remember one thing ~ that when an angel speaks, it is the same as God speaking. When God is speaking through angels, He does not give angels an opportunity to change His own words and interject their own thoughts. The angel is speaking the exact words of God as He spoke them Himself! That's why God can trust them and that's why He has trusted them on so many tremendous occasions.

When The Angels Were Powerless

When Jesus went to the cross, He took upon Himself all the sins of the world, all the filth and all the sickness, all the disease, all the vile things that everyone in the entire world has ever done. Then He went down into the very pit of hell, and came out victorious! As He hung on the cross and as He went into hell, God's angels were powerless to do anything for Him because God had not given them any instructions!

The sky must have been full of angels all the time. Consequently I'm sure that the angels were there while all this was going on, and yet they were completely bound. They could not do anything because God had not given them any orders. So they, like every person there, stood by and watched Jesus be crucified on the cross.

Now watch what happened when Jesus came back to life, when He arose for the dead! The great message of all times concerning the resurrection was entrusted to an angel to tell.

Now after the Sabbath, as the first day of the week began to dawn, Mary Magdalene and the other Mary came to see the tomb.

And behold, there was a great earthquake; for an angel of the Lord descended from heaven, and came and rolled back the stone from the door, and sat on it (Matthew 28:2).

I can just picture the guards who had made sure that the tomb was sealed with a stone and had watchmen around it all the time! Angels have personalities and I can just picture this angel sitting on that stone laughing and laughing and saying, "Oh, wait until the priests find out what happened."

This angel sat there on the stone just to watch and see, even though they knew what was going to happen next.

He had been in the very presence of God! When Moses was up on the Mount of Transfiguration and came down, the glory of the Lord was upon him. The glory of the Lord was on the angel, that's why

his countenance was like lightning and his clothing as white as snow (Matthew 28:3).

And the guards shook for fear of him, and became like dead men (Matthew 28:4).

They fell under the power of God. I believe that is exactly the same thing you and I would have done if we had been sent there to guard the tomb of the man who had just been hung on a cross and suddenly we discovered that the stone had been rolled away and the tomb was empty! The angel didn't tell the guards not to be afraid.

But the angel answered and said to the women, "Do not be afraid, for I know that you seek Jesus who was crucified" (Matthew 28:5).

Do Not Be Afraid

Notice that to those who are on God's side the angels always say, *"Do not be afraid."* Don't be frightened.

He wants to put us at ease. I imagine if we could see into the face of an angel we would see something that would bring peace and comfort to our hearts!

He is not here; for He is risen. Three of those words have come down through history! On every newspaper in the land, probably in almost every country around the world, on Easter Sunday, those three words appear, *"HE IS RISEN."*

They were direct words from God to the people, spoken through an angel, *"He is risen!"* Jesus didn't stay in that tomb. He arose. Hallelujah!

"Come, see the place where the Lord lay. And go quickly and tell His disciples that He is risen from the dead, and indeed He is going before you into Galilee; there you will see Him! Behold I have told you."

So they departed quickly from the tomb with fear and great joy, and ran to bring His disciples word (Matthew 28:6-8).

Isn't that interesting? Did you notice that it did say they departed quickly from the tomb with fear even though the angels had told them not to have fear. They really took off because I believe they knew that they had received a message from the Almighty God to go and tell the others, *"He is risen!"*

We were in Dallas, Texas, one week speaking at a church. This was the last night and just before we began to minister to those who were sick, more than eight hundred angels came into this church. Previously we had never seen so many angels all at one time! They were different than the angel which is stationed with us all the time.

These were what I would call blessing angels. They were probably four-and-a-half to five feet tall. They were all grouped together in little covies with five or six of them in each. During the praise time of the service they were all worshipping and praising God. I could see them clapping their hands like they were saying, "Oh, glory hallelujah! Here is a church that really knows how to praise God. Here are some people who really know how to praise God."

The reason that I say more than eight hundred angels is because there were approximately eight hundred people in the church and there were more angels than there were people. Then a very interesting thing began to happen. I watched groups of angels go down to certain people and they brought them forward to the altar. As they were brought forward by the angels they were healed, not by the angels but by the power of God.

I especially remember one young couple had a little baby who had a hole in the heart and a heart murmur. The husband was not holding the baby, the wife was. He told us later he had reached over, because his hands were absolutely forced out by the angels, picked the baby up and came to the altar. He looked completely dazed as he handed the baby to us. We prayed and then handed the baby back to him totally healed!

The angels nudged him to reach over and pick up that baby and he did! They took the baby back to the doctor and the doctor said the heart murmur and the hole in the heart were totally and completely healed!

Special note: We recently attended this *healthy* young man's graduation from high school!

CHAPTER 7

There Are Two Kinds Of Angels

Do you know there are two kinds of angels?

Holy angels and demon angels...

No sooner had the thought entered Satan's mind, "...I want to be like God," until he found himself thrown out of heaven. Because God cannot stand sin, the moment that thought started to enter Lucifer's mind, the devil was cast out of heaven like a bolt of lightning and on this same bolt of lightning there were one-third of all the angels in heaven cast out along with Lucifer.

And He (Jesus) said to them, "I saw Satan fall like lightning from Heaven" (Luke 10:18).

As this bolt of lightning zoomed through space, it carried all of these demonic angels who were no longer holy angels but had become evil angels! Can you imagine the storm that was created as this heavenly missile hurtled through the earth's atmosphere? The sound must have been horrible. The once-beautiful voice of Lucifer, the most magnificent voice in all of heaven had now changed to a hideous scream as he was cast at a supernatural speed to his unholy destiny. He could no longer be called Lucifer, a praiser of God. He became Satan, the devil!

Even as the angels were cast down, their character changed. They were no longer holy angels from God, but became part of the devil's kingdom, the evil angels.

No one knows the total number of angels in heaven. In the book of Revelation, John refers to the angels around the throne as being ten-thousand times ten-thousand plus thousands and thousands. There must have been multitudes of angels who were cast out. Imagine the hideous screams as these beings realized they would no longer be comfortably nested in heaven, but were instead cast down to earth, and ultimately into the bottomless pit.

Imagine the commotion that was created when this bolt of lightning carrying all of these demonic creatures landed on earth! Ever since that time they have continued to carry out that same confusion and commotion!

We have found the notes on demons in the *Life Application Bible* to be so helpful in this study that we have included them below.

What Are Demons?

A man possessed by a demon was present and began shouting, "Why are you bothering us, Jesus of Nazareth ~ have you come to destroy us demons? I know who you are ~ the holy Son of

God!" Jesus curtly commanded the demon to say no more and to come out of the man. At that the evil spirit screamed and convulsed the man violently and left him (Mark 1:23-26).

Demons are evil spirits who are ruled by Satan. They work to tempt people to sin. They were not created by Satan, because God is the Creator of all; rather they are fallen angels who joined Satan in his rebellion. In their degenerate state they can cause a person to become mute, deaf, blind or insane. But in every case where they confronted Jesus, they lost their power. Thus God limits what they can do; they can do nothing without his permission. During Jesus' life on earth demons were allowed to be very active to show once and for all Christ's power and authority over them.

Many psychologists dismiss accounts of demon possession as a primitive way to describe mental illness. Clearly, however, a demon controlled the man described in Mark 1:23. Mark emphasizes Jesus' conflict with evil powers to show his superiority over them, and so he records many stories about Jesus casting out demons. Jesus didn't have to conduct an elaborate exorcism ritual. His word was enough to send out the demons.

The demon mentioned above knew at once that Jesus was the Son of God. Mark, by including this event in this Gospel was establishing Jesus' credentials, showing that even the underworld recognized Jesus as the Messiah.

Why Didn't Jesus Destroy The Demons?

Jesus healed many people of the destructive work of demon-possession, but He did not destroy the demons. Why didn't Jesus destroy or stop the evil in the world? His time for that has not yet come. But it will. The book of Revelation records the future victory of Jesus over Satan, all his demons and all evil.

The Demon Recognized Jesus

When they arrived at the other side of the lake a demon-possessed man ran out from a graveyard, just as Jesus was climbing from the boat. This man lived among the gravestones, and had such strength that whenever he was put into hand-cuffs and shackles ~ as he often was ~ he snapped the handcuffs from his wrists and smashed the shackles and walked away. No one was strong enough to control him. All day long and through the night he would wander among the tombs and in the wild hills, screaming and cutting himself with sharp pieces of stone.

When Jesus was still far out on the water, the man had seen him and had run to meet him, and fell down before him. Then Jesus spoke to the demon within the man and said, "Come out, you evil spirit."
It gave a terrible scream, shrieking, "What are you going to do to me, Jesus, Son of the Most High God? For God's sake, don't torture me!"

More Than One Demon

"What is your name," Jesus asked, and the demon replied, "Legion, for there are many of us here within this man." Then the demons begged him again and again not to send them to some distant land.

Into A Herd Of Hogs

Now as it happened there was a huge herd of hogs rooting around on the hill above the lake. "Send us into those hogs," the demons begged. And Jesus gave them permission. Then the evil spirits came out of the man and entered the hogs, and the entire herd plunged down the steep hillside into the lake and drowned.

The People Ask Jesus To Leave

The herdsmen fled to the nearby towns and countryside, spreading the news as they ran. Everyone rushed out to see for themselves. And a large crowd soon gathered where Jesus was; but as they saw the man sitting there, fully clothed and perfectly sane, they were frightened. Those who saw what happened were telling everyone about it, and the crowd began pleading with Jesus to go away and leave them alone! (Mark 5:1-17).

The demons destroyed the pigs and hurt the herdsmen's finances, but can pigs and money compare to human life? A man had been freed from the devil's power, but the villagers thought only about their pocketbooks. People have always tended to value personal gain over other people. Throughout history most wars have been fought, at least in part, to protect economic interests. Much injustice and oppression, both at home and abroad, is the direct fallout of some individual's or company's urge to get rich. People are continually being sacrificed to money. Don't think more highly of "pigs" than of people. Think carefully about how your decisions will affect other human beings, and be willing to choose a simpler lifestyle if it would keep other people from being harmed.

The Power Of Demons

Once as he was teaching in the synagogue, a man possessed by a demon began shouting at Jesus, "Go away! We want nothing to do with you, Jesus from Nazareth. You have come to destroy us. I know who you are ~ the Holy Son of God." Jesus cut him short. "Be silent!" he told the demon. "Come out!" The demon threw the man to the floor as the crowd watched, and then left him without hurting him further (Luke 4:33-35).

The Goal of Demons

The book of Mark often highlights the supernatural struggle between Jesus and Satan. The demons' goal was to control the humans they inhabited; Jesus' goal was to give people freedom from sin and Satan's control. The demons knew they had no power over Jesus, so when they saw him, they begged not to be sent to a distant land (called the Bottomless Pit in Luke 8:31). Jesus granted their request but ended their destructive work in people. He could have sent them to hell, but he did not because the time for judgment had not yet come. In the end, of course, all demons will be sent into eternal fire.

The people were amazed at Jesus' authority to cast out demons ~ evil spirits ruled by Satan and sent to tempt people to sin. Demons can cause a person to become mute, deaf, blind or insane. Jesus faced many demons during his time on earth and he always exerted authority over them. Not only did the demon leave this man; Luke records that the man was not even hurt.

The Ultimate Fate Of Demons

They began screaming at him, "What do you want with us, O Son of God? You have no right to torment us yet" (Matthew 8:29).

The Bible tells us that at the end of the world, Satan and his angels will be thrown into the Lake of Fire. When the demons said that Jesus could not torment them ˝yet,˝ they showed they knew their ultimate fate.

Demon Possession And Its Purpose

Although we cannot be sure why demon possession occurs, we know that it uses the body in a destructive way to distort and destroy man's relationship with God and likeness to him. Even today, demons are dangerous, powerful and destructive. While it is important to recognize their evil activity so we can stay away from them, we must avoid any curiosity about or involvement with demonic forces or the occult. If we resist the devil and his influences, he will flee from us.

So give yourselves humbly to God. Resist the devil and he will flee from you (James 4:7).

Jesus' Power And Authority Over Demons

[Satan must be bound before his demons are cast out], just as a strong man must be tied up before his house can be ransacked and his property robbed (Mark 3:27).

Although God permits Satan to work in our world, God is still in control. Jesus, because He is God, has power over Satan; he is able to cast out demons and end their terrible work in people's lives. One day Satan will be bound forever, never again to do this evil work in the world (end of note from Life Application Bible).

Jesus Defeated The Devil 2,000 Years Ago

We felt we could not write a book about the holy angels unless we wrote about demonic angels as well. Jesus defeated the devil and all his demons 2,000 years ago. We personally do not spend much of our time talking about demonic spirits. We believe that every time we talk about evil we're taking away from the time that we're talking about Jesus. However, it is important to know that demons have a place in the world today. We need to learn how to stand against them.

In any study of demons, it is good to remember John's words, *You are of God, little children, and have overcome them, because He who is in you is greater than he who is in the world* (I John 4:4).

We like to quote this verse saying, *Greater is He that is in me than he that is in the world.* He that is in this world includes the devil and every one of his demons.

Standing Against Evil Angels

Put on the whole armor of God, that you may be able to stand against the wiles of the devil. For we do not wrestle against flesh and blood, but against principalities, against powers, against the rulers of the darkness of this age, against spiritual hosts of wickedness in the heavenly places. (Ephesians 6:11,12).

And don't ever take that armor off!

We fight against fallen angels over whom Satan has control. They are very real and we face a powerful army whose goal is to defeat Christ's church. We know that Jesus will win in the end, but we must engage in the battle until Jesus comes because Satan is constantly battling against every born-again believer. To defeat him, we must have supernatural power because he is a supernatural enemy. God provides us with this power through the baptism with the Holy Spirit.

Always remember that you have more power than the devil. In Matthew 28:18, Jesus said, *All authority has been given to Me in heaven and on earth.*

Jesus had all power, but then He displayed true Christianity ~ He gave it away to us, so we would have more power than the devil.

And in Luke 10:19 He said, *Behold I give you the authority to trample on serpents and scorpions, and over all the power of the enemy, and nothing shall by any means hurt you.*

In Jesus, we have more power than the enemy. He is a defeated foe! We are more than conquerors through Him who loved us!

CHAPTER 8

Angels Come In Different Colors

Colombia, the nation most widely known because it is the largest producer of drugs of any country in the world, is also loaded with angels!

During a Healing Explosion there, the sponsor anticipated so many people attending that he scheduled two piggyback services.

We had spent an incredible week training the people how to minister healing to the sick! We were told that over six thousand had signed up to take the final training. The sponsoring pastor had to reduce the number to fifteen hundred and each seat was at a premium. The coffee companies brought coffee wagons to the scene, and everyone received free Colombian coffee!

Then came the day of the actual Healing Explosion. There was a supernatural atmosphere in the morning service, but even this did not prepare us completely for what was to happen.

After we ministered to several people on the stage, we released the healing teams to go into the audience and lay hands on the sick, which they did with incredible results!

The second service started, and the pastor walked over to the two of us and said, "I believe God would like for you to lay hands on those in wheelchairs this time!" We looked at the audience and saw about three rows of wheelchairs all around the inside area of the auditorium floor. They do not have medicare and hospitalization like we have in the United States so you see many more hopeless cripples than we see here.

We started to say, "We came here to teach your people how to heal the sick," but didn't because we realized this was a special request from this beautiful pastor. As we walked down the stairs Charles and I both looked up and said, "God if you're not in this we're sunk!" But if God isn't in any Healing Explosion, we're already sunk!

We know just a tiny little bit of Spanish and the only thing we really knew to say was, "Recibe su sanidad en el nombre de Jesús," which means, "Receive your healing in the Name of Jesus." We didn't ask them what their problem was because that gets too complicated when you try to translate it from Spanish to English.

We walked up to the first person in a wheelchair, a hopelessly crippled man, laid hands on him and said, "Recibe su sanidad en el nombre de Jesús!"

Acts 3:6 is a scripture we usually say when we lay hands on someone in a wheelchair.

"Silver and gold I do not have, but what I do have I give you: In the name of Jesus Christ of Nazareth, rise up and walk."

This is one of the few scriptures I know in Spanish, so I quoted it until I got to the very last four words. *Rise up and walk* and my mind went completely blank ~ completely and totally blank! I remembered the word for *rise up* but I could not remember the word for *walk* in Spanish. It had totally vanished from my mind! I quickly searched all through my memory, but that word would not come into my mind, but God...

It is amazing how quickly and interestingly God can insert thoughts into our spirit and into our minds. He reminded me of a little song we had sung as children. This is a song I think almost everybody knows, "La cucaracha, la cucaracha, ya no puede caminar..." "The cockroach, the cockroach, now he is unable to *walk...*" There was the word I needed ~ caminar ~ "to walk" and God put it back into my mind in the most peculiar way!

In the event you don't know the rest of the words of that song in Spanish they are, "Porque le falta, porque no tiene, marijuana que fumar," which means he can't walk because he lacks, because he doesn't have, marijuana to smoke!

What a peculiar way for God to remind me of something! He knew that was one way I would instantly know the Spanish word for "to walk."

We looked at the man and said, "Levantase y camina

en el nombre de Jesús!" which means, "Rise up and walk in the Name of Jesus."

The minute we said that the man got up from his wheelchair and walked!

I was startled! I looked at Charles and said, "He must not have been as crippled as we thought he was," but we were rejoicing.

If something is successful, do it again! We went to the second person who was also hopelessly crippled and said the same thing. We had no sooner said, "Get up and walk," than he got right up out of his wheelchair and walked!

This was exciting! We continued making the same anointed commands in Jesus' Name. We went down the line and the first sixteen people got out of their wheelchairs and walked! When we got to number seventeen we couldn't believe it. The man sat there and didn't get up! We weren't discouraged! We went on to number eighteen and before we made the circle, over one hundred people had either gotten out of their wheelchairs, off of stretchers, or off of crutches. One blind man was instantly healed. What a day of glory!

How we praised the Lord! God sent us a real anointed helper! There was a beautiful black man there with a tremendous amount of gray hair! This is very unusual because most black African people never really get a lot of gray in their hair. As soon as we had told the first man to get up and walk, this big black man walked over and took his arm and walked him out to the center of the arena. While he was walking him out there we could hear him encouraging the man in Spanish who came out of the wheelchair probably saying something like, "That's right! That's right! Keep walking because you have to get your muscles strengthened." He was exhorting him to put his faith into action and continue walking so he wouldn't lose his healing. What a blessing!

When we finished ministering to the second person, the man quickly returned and took that person and escorted him out to the center of the arena apparently with the same encouraging words he had given to the first one. Without exception, every person who got out of a wheelchair was ministered to by this beautiful black man with the gray curly hair. He had to have supernatural ability to be able to move so quickly!

The last twenty people got out of their wheelchairs and came up to us and said, "Would you please lay hands on us?" They hadn't even realized the power of God was so strong that they were already healed!

As you can imagine, everybody was sobbing because of the mighty move of God. We had never seen anything like that before, nor have we ever seen anything like that since! It was an extremely emotional moment.

I ran up to get to the stage where my purse was and my daughter said, "Don't look in there for Kleenex! They're all used up!" Many people later told us they had never seen such a dramatic service in their entire life!

After we regained our composure a little bit, we released the healing teams to minister healing to everybody else. We saw the black man leaving ~ he just disappeared into the crowd before I could say anything to him. We ran over to the pastor and asked, "Who is that black man? He did such a wonderful job helping us by exhorting those people and exercising them so they would continue walking. We want to thank him."

The pastor said, "I didn't see anybody."

We said, "The big black man who was helping us." He was at least a foot taller than Charles who is six feet tall.

The pastor said again, "I didn't see him!"

Many other people gave the same answer!

But our camera saw him and surprisingly, he appears in many of our snapshots! The video camera caught him as well!

God will send His angelic messengers to give you all the help you need even if others can't see him!

This was one of God's invisible angels, but made visible to us and to our cameras!

Glory to God!

CHAPTER 9

Angel Vignettes

INTRODUCTION

We could fill volumes relating the wonderful things God has done for us through His ministering angels. We could write story after story, ours and our friends, about angelic visitations to us. But our desire in writing this book is not to entertain with marvelous accounts of angelic visitation in our own lives, but to create within you a desire to experience more of the supernatural power of God. The more we share about personal encounters in our lives and ministry, the more real is our relationship with God and Jesus!

As you have been reading the accounts in this book, you may have been thinking about an experience you or a friend have had. Were angels involved in your own life? If you have never considered it in that way, take time to do so now and thank God for every remembrance He gives you.

King Solomon wrote,

Trust in the LORD with all your heart, and lean

*not on your own understanding; in all your ways
acknowledge Him, and He shall direct your paths*
(Proverbs 3:5,6).

Take time to thank God for the supernatural intervention He has already given you, and ask Him for more.

Angels Visited Charles' Mother
By Frances

Charles said, "I don't even remember the first encounter I personally had with angels!" I thought, "How
could you ever forget anything as exciting as a live encounter with an angel?"

I quickly found out!

Because of our tremendous interest in angels and
the intense studies we were making at the time, God
brought back to our minds several sheets of paper written by Charles' mother. She was a true saint of God if I
ever saw one! We had a letter dated June 15, 1969 in
which she wrote, "I really would like to tell you about
some of the visions I had, so I wrote them on paper.
They are not as good as if I told them because I just am
not able to put in words what I want to when I start to
write. Maybe you can say them better than I and yet still
have the same meaning." The paper had a headline in
mama's handwriting.

*"My visions of angels bringing our boy, Charles,
to me."*
*"The night before he was born I saw a group of
angels coming down over my bed and one said,*

*'This is your beloved son.' They had a bundle
they handed to me and then they were gone.*"

What an awesome thing it was when I read her words.
It was a reminder to me that we must more fully realize
that supernatural angelic activities are happening all the
time in our own lives!

God put a call on Charles' life even before he was
actually born, or possibly at the very moment he was
born!

Charles' mama knew this but kept it in her heart
until a few months before God joined us in marriage.

Charles said, "I never went far away from God (just
a few bad attitudes) but I remember something I did as
a teenager. My parents were devout Christians and I
knew they didn't want me to go to a movie. But I did. I
'sneaked away' and thoroughly enjoyed a clean movie.
Somehow I believe my mother knew, but she also some
way knew that I had a God-given call on my life. I
couldn't and didn't get away from God. Finally He put
a divine hook in my jaw and reeled me into the kingdom of God. After I made a total commitment, an aban-
donment of my life, that ended my desire to sin, even a
little bit!"

Maybe an angel didn't bring a special package to
you, but God has a call on every life He chooses!

Isaiah wrote,

*"Everyone who is called by My glory; I have
formed him, yes, I have made him"* (Isaiah 43:7).

Seeing Angels in the Spirit
By Charles

Angels can be seen just like we see a human or they can be seen in any dimension God wants them to be.

They can appear large.

They can appear small.

They can come in the form of a male or female, or as a child.

God has them appear in whatever form necessary in order to fulfill their purpose at that time. They are not restricted to our human vision.

One morning we were ministering on a stage in a large auditorium. I was talking at that time and Frances was seated possibly twenty or thirty feet over to my left listening to what I was saying. Suddenly I stopped and said, "Frances, I want to tell the people where our big angel is."

Frances was rather shocked by that and she thought to herself, "God, let him be in the spirit because he can't see the angel the way he's standing." She had seen this heavenly presence physically standing just in front of the drapes in back of me and she knew I couldn't see out of the back of my head.

I was looking directly into the face of the audience and I didn't change my position at all when I began to describe where the angel was. I said, "The angel is standing directly in back of me. He is just barely in front of the drapes. He's looking over my head right into the faces of the people in the audience."

Frances breathed a sigh of relief as she realized that God had shown me, even though she knew I couldn't see him, exactly what she was watching and seeing clearly.

That caused us to realize that you don't have to limit God in any way with or without angels. It was very clear that I was seeing him in my spirit but I wasn't looking at him as we would look at another human being. In the spirit visibility can be any part of 360 degrees, any height or depth, even through wood or steel. Hallelujah!

Moving in the spirit, I had "eyes in the back of my head!"

Angels Give Heart's Desires
By Charles

A church in Wichita Falls reserved the front pew for our family who had accompanied us to a meeting we were having there. I was sitting about three feet from the end of the pew, not even thinking about angels. Our plane had been delayed, so things had been a little hectic. I decided to completely enter into the worship service because there is nothing that will calm you down after a hectic rough airplane flight like worshiping God, so I really became involved in doing just that.

I opened my eyes and looked at the stage and was thrilled and surprised to sense our huge angel standing there. It was a real comforting feeling! There's a dimension similar to a magnetic field and I could see the angel clearly in the spirit even though I couldn't see him physically. He was standing on the stage looking at the congregation.

I prayed silently, "Father, it sure would be nice if

you would let him move down here and sit next to us on the front pew!" I hadn't even had time to blink my eyes when the angel instantly left the stage and was standing next to me!

As I stood there I could clearly tell the whole height and features of this great angel. I'm almost six feet tall, but he was almost eight feet tall! My head was at the middle of his forearm. He totally dwarfed me.

God had instantly responded to a little thought request of mine and honored it by sending the angel down to sit with us. What a blessing!

Take delight in the Lord, and he will give you your heart's desires (Psalm 37:4 NLT).

Angels Give Strength
By Charles and Frances

An unusual thing happened in a California service. At the very beginning of this meeting, a blonde boy about eleven or twelve years old fell out under the power of the Holy Spirit.

The minute he fell on the floor, his arms went right straight up in the air! As the service progressed, we noticed that he never moved and that his arms were staying in the same position ~ straight up in the air! This went on for approximately three hours, the entire length of the service. During this time many people noticed this unusual phenomenon! When his arms finally came down, we ran over to him!

We were amazed that he could hold his arms up for such a long time, so we said to him, "Didn't your arms get tired holding them up that long?"

He said excitedly, "No, they didn't get tired! Didn't you see the angels? There was one on each side and they held my arms up the entire time. That's why they didn't get tired!"

That was about twenty-four years ago. How we would love to see that young man today to find out what that angelic visitation did in his life!

Angels Bring Healing
By Frances

This angel has appeared and still appears many times in our meetings or other places. I have never talked to him and I do not see him all the time. But on the special occasions when I do see him, something unusual always happens in the audience.

At one meeting where this mighty angel appeared, there was a man in the congregation who seemed to be unusually tense. We were very much aware of him because it was as if the Holy Spirit had shined a bright light on him. He later spoke to us and said he felt like his head was going to burst, or he was an applicant for a stroke, or something equally as dramatic and traumatic.

At one point I had looked out and had seen the angel ministering to this particular man and I knew there was a miracle in the making!

He said, "The minute I silently expressed what I felt, I felt somebody laid a hand on me and, whatever the problem was, it absolutely totally and completely disappeared!"

God answered this man's cry by sending a special angel right to his seat!

Angels Protect Us From Accidents
By Frances

Praise the Lord that angels are given charge over us!

As we were being driven from our hotel to the site of a meeting in Canada, we proceeded through a green light but the person driving a van coming from the other direction ran through their red light and obviously didn't see us.

We were in an ordinary automobile, when the driver of the van proceeded through the red light ~ drove right toward the engine of our car and went right straight through it! I was sitting in the front seat and even though the motor extended way out in front of our car, the driver's face was no more than six or eight inches from the windshield of the car in which we were riding!

The van proceeded down the street, but not for long! The people climbed out of the car with the most shocked looks on their faces we've ever seen. They were looking to see what had happened to their vehicle but there was nothing the matter! We all said the same thing, "Did you see that angel?"

An angel somehow supernaturally let that van run right through the motor of our car with no damage whatsoever! There was no accident, no clanging of metal, no jarring, no nothing.

Jesus Walked Through Walls

Then, the same day at evening, being the first

*day of the week, when the doors were shut where
the disciples were assembled, for fear of the Jews,
Jesus came and stood in the midst, and said to
them, "Peace be with you"* (John 20:19).

Angels are a blessing. They protect us from harm!

Angels Guard Our Possessions
By Frances

The life of evangelists is oftentimes fraught with many
interesting and unexpected events. At a Canadian meeting,
our books and video tapes were displayed in the
vestibule of the church but the actual service was in the
fellowship hall which was slightly removed from the vestibule,
leaving the book table completely unattended until
the conclusion of the meeting. As we were ministering,
we were not concerned about the books and videos even
though there is a lot of money involved producing these
items.

I was not even aware that anything was happening,
but toward the end of the service a young man ran up,
put his arms around me, squeezed me tightly and started
crying! I said, "What's the matter?" It was obvious he
needed to be saved, or that he had some sort of physical
or overwhelming personal problem he needed to discuss.

Imagine my surprise when he replied, "I was driving
by and saw all those books by the door and realized
I could sell them for a lot of money, so I came in and
stole a whole bunch of them! After I drove away, the
funniest thing happened to me. An angel came and told

me to take all the books and videos back. I was afraid not to, so here they are!"

I said, "You need to be saved!"

He said, "I know it!" And he got saved right on the spot!

But angels are only servants. They are spirits sent from God to care for those who will receive salvation (Hebrews 1:14 NLT).

Angels Guard Our Home
By Charles

Christmas is a wonderful time to have special friends and loved ones in to sing carols and worship God together. One night during the time we had a Bible school at the City of Light, we invited all our students to come to our home to celebrate Jesus!

Frances and I went up to the balcony of our home overlooking the living room. We were standing possibly three feet apart, which is unusual for us because we normally stand right together, but we soon discovered the reason!

The students were all singing Christmas carols and we all had our hands raised in the air when suddenly the big angel who watches over us came and stood between us. The three of us were looking down over the Bible school students. The students saw him first and they thought it was an awesome thing to realize that God's special warrior angel was visible in our home.

None of them will ever be the same!

When we moved out of our previous home, a real

estate friend was selling our house. He said that almost everyone who looked at the house said, "What is this we feel?"

Our agent replied, "I don't know, but these people *sure are religious!*"

When we moved out, we had asked God to station angels over that home to protect it and to guard it. God answered our prayer, and though they didn't know it they were actually sensing the presence of angels who were watching over the house!

Praise the Lord, our angel moved with us, but God stationed others to guard our house until it sold!

Angels Lift Us Up
By Frances

Do you have any idea what it feels like to get hit with bursitis in the hip and have to be taken from an airplane to a car, driven across an airfield, put in a wheelchair and taken upstairs to be put on another plane so that you can get home? I should add, **especially** when you're in the healing ministry!

I had been attacked with bursitis in my hip while we were on a ministry trip and was totally unable to walk! When we got to Atlanta, Charles called our office and told them to make a doctor's appointment quickly!

We always pray first, but we know God also uses doctors, so our secretary picked us up and took us directly to the doctor's office. He promptly gave me a shot of cortisone in my hip, but missed the joint just a little bit, so it didn't knock the bursitis out.

They loaned me a wheelchair to get back to our car. Our secretary had gone back to work, so Charles was going to drive us home. Charles is an excellent driver, but this afternoon he was not driving very well. When we turned the final corner to go toward our condo, I was aware that he wasn't driving normally at all. I said, "Charles, is something the matter with you?"

He said, "Sweetheart, I am so sick I need to get home and in bed as fast as I can!" He had been so concerned about me, he hadn't realized how badly he felt.

I limped into the condo as fast as I could with my hip in agony and we both went to bed because neither of us was able to do very much!

Shortly after this I took Charles' temperature and discovered it was over 102 degrees! My bursitis was so painful that I could hardly get out of bed, but I remembered we had some antibiotics which the doctor had given us to take overseas in the event we picked up any kind of disease or infection. I said to Charles, "Let me give you one of those pills."

The way I got out of bed to get the pill was really something! I was hanging onto everything within my reach because I couldn't stand because of the pain in my hip! He took the antibiotic and we went to sleep.

Somewhere around three o'clock in the morning I woke up and reached over to give Charles a "love pat" (which I always do when I wake up during the night) and discovered he wasn't there! I had not heard him get up, which was unusual, and I almost panicked! I thought, "Surely he didn't rapture without me!" No, I decided he's probably in the bathroom so I rolled over and went back to sleep.

About thirty minutes later, I woke up and once again reached over in the bed to give him a "love pat" but he still wasn't there. It was a horrible feeling! Somehow in my spirit I knew too much time had elapsed and that something must be wrong. Either that or the Holy Spirit nudged me and told me something was wrong, so I called out, "Charles, where are you?"

"I'm in the bathroom," came his weak answer.

I said, "What are you doing in there?"

He very calmly replied, "I'm sitting on the floor."

The minute he said, "Sitting on the floor," I knew something was wrong! Charles' normal behavior does not include sitting on the bathroom floor! In spite of the painful bursitis, it is amazing the strength the Holy Spirit or angels gave me, so I jumped out of bed and ran into the bathroom.

When I say I ran into the bathroom, that is a very poor description of what I actually did. The bursitis was so painful I had to hang onto every piece of furniture between my side of the bed and the bathroom to even get there, but God increased my adrenaline enough for me to make it!

When I saw Charles, I could not believe my eyes! He was sitting on the floor in a totally dazed condition. Blood was squirting from his head and covering his pajamas, the rugs, and the floor!

I screamed, "What happened?"

He answered, "I remember falling and my head hitting the floor, but that's all."

I asked, "Can you roll over on your hands and knees and crawl back to bed after I get this blood cleaned up?"

I didn't know how I was going to get it cleaned up because I couldn't even bend over myself!

He tried to get on his knees but he couldn't even lift the fingers of his left hand.

He couldn't move anything except for a little wiggle in one finger. He didn't know what damage had been done to his spine!

Normally I am the type of person who knows immediately what to do in a situation like this, but I really fell apart and said, "Charles, what shall we do? I can't carry you back to bed!

"Should I call Barbara (that's our secretary)?"

Then I said, "Should I call 911?"

Then I said, "Should I call the hospital?"

We had no idea what to do because I couldn't walk with the horrible bursitis in my hip, and Charles certainly couldn't walk, and there was no way I could get him back to bed!

At exactly the same moment, both of us put in a 911 call to heaven. We only said two words, "Jesus, help!"

I would like to tell you what happened next...

...but I can't.

I have no recollection of getting the blood off of Charles! I did not clean up the floor because I was totally incapable of doing that, but the next thing either of us remember was that the next morning we awoke at the same time and both of us were in bed. I said to

Charles, "How did you get in bed?"

He said, "I don't know. How did you get in bed?"

I said, "I don't know."

We looked at the bed. We looked at the floor. We got up and looked at the bathroom and there was not a sign of blood anywhere.

How did that happen?

There is only one answer!

We believe with our hearts and souls that an angel picked us both up; put us back in our bed and washed the blood off Charles and cleaned up the rest of the mess for us.

The only thing he had showing the next morning was a badly skinned head and the blackest eye we have ever seen in all of our life!

Praise the Lord that He gives His angels charge over us ~ even an extra love touch in cleaning the house for us!

Because you have made the Lord, who is my ref-
-uge, even the Most High, your habitation,
No evil shall befall you, Nor shall any plague
come near your dwelling;
For He shall give His angels charge over you, to
keep you in all your ways (Psalm 91:9-12).

An Invisible Orchestra
By Charles

Will angels be visible to more of the body of Christ in the end-time church than in the early church? About one-third of all mentions of angels in the Bible is in the book of Revelation, and we believe that is the day in which we are now living!

In recent years hundreds of people have come to us with testimonies of seeing angels or having had visits by angels. The exciting thing about some of these witnesses is that we have seen the angels appear in the same place they tell of seeing them, and they describe the angels exactly as we have seen them. God does confirm His word by many witnesses.

Shortly after we received the baptism with the Holy Spirit, we were ministering in a miracle service in Austin, Texas. Frances and I, the worship leader and another man were on the stage of the auditorium. During the beautiful worship, Frances turned to the worship leader and said, "Will you lead us in singing in the Spirit?" He looked rather shocked that she would make such an earthly request for such a heavenly act as singing in the Spirit. A lot of Spirit-filled believers had not yet discovered you can sing in the Spirit at any time, and do not have to wait until the "Spirit comes on you!"

Just before the worship leader started to lead the singing in tongues, we heard a sound which made us both instantly turn toward the piano.

Coming from that direction, we heard what sounded like a thousand piece orchestra tuning their instruments just before a concert. But ~ the piano bench was empty and a guitar was resting beside the bench! The volume began to intensify as they seemed ready for the downbeat of the orchestra leader. Then simultaneously with the worship leader starting to sing in the Spirit, the whole invisible orchestra played in harmony with this beautiful singing in tongues. We heard the music of a thousand angels and it was awesome!

Angels in Witnessing
By Charles and Frances

Angels have a multifaceted job, and to make a job description of all the things they do would be very difficult. We just try to be ready for whatever happens when they make an appearance!

At all times there is a burning desire in our hearts for people to witness for Jesus! Over the years, this is one of the subjects we have brought up at almost every one of our services. We are always amazed because so many people have a genuine fear of witnessing ~ fear of rejection or failure.

A young man recently said to me,

"There may be a million reasons why people don't witness for Jesus but here are the three most popular ones.

"The first reason is that Christians do not have a real concept of what heaven and hell are. The Bible tells us that heaven is where we will see Jesus face to face. It is a beautiful place where there will be no sickness or poverty. However, since we may be living a real good life here, it's possible just the idea of heaven will not encourage us to tell people about Jesus.

"If we really understand what hell is like, it will encourage us to share Jesus with everybody we meet. We should visualize hell and envision our own mother there because we didn't talk to her about Jesus. (I have often said that God gave me a vision of what hell was like the day I got saved and that is why I don't want anyone to go there!)

He continued,

"We know we are not allowed to kill, lie, steal, have sex outside of marriage. Those are God's commandments. But Jesus' last commandment is the Great Commission. He said we are to "*go into all the world and preach the gospel to every creature.*" If we take this commandment to heart and witness in every opportunity to everyone we meet, we will be fulfilling the number one commandment. "*And you shall love the Lord your God with all your heart, with all your soul, with all your mind, and with all your strength.' This is the first commandment. And the second, like it, is this: 'You shall love your neighbor as your-self.' There is no other commandment greater than these*" (Mark 12:30,31).

"The second reason for not witnessing is that we have not taken this as a commandment. We have taken it as a suggestion. Many people say, 'I'm not called to be an evangelist.' Jesus was sent to earth for one purpose, 'to save the lost.' He gave His life in a horrible way to provide for us a way to come into a relationship with God. His last instructions to His disciples whom He left in charge just before He went back to heaven was to *"preach the gospel to every creature"* (Mark 16:15). It is our responsibility as soon as we are saved to tell somebody about our experience no matter how we say it. The apostle Paul wrote, *That if you confess with your mouth the Lord Jesus and believe in your heart that God has raised Him from the dead, you will be saved* (Rom. 10:9).

"Remember the rich man who went to hell? It wasn't until he got to hell that he had a heart for missions. Once he was there he said to Abraham, *'Why don't you send people to my relatives?'* Isn't it a shame for someone to have to go to hell before becoming mission minded?

"The third hindrance to witnessing is devil-instigated fear. The Bible tells us that *there is no fear in love; but perfect love casts out fear* (I John 4:18). The fear of rejection and of failure causes even long-time seasoned Christians to literally 'freeze up' when an opportunity confronts them."

Jesus' command: *"Preach the gospel to every creature."*

"FEAR!" is the response of so many Christians.

During a meeting in Massachusettes, I was teaching the people to start witnessing without fear. At God's leading, I commanded the spirit of fear to come out of every person there and for a spirit of boldness to come into everyone!

Then...

Standing in military-like formation, shoulder-to-shoulder along both sides and across the back of the auditorium appeared rows of giant angels dressed like warriors! It was a formidable sight because the angels were pressed so tightly against one another that nothing could possibly get through that wall of warriors! Both of us saw this clearly!

Then God gave me a prophetic message for the people: "Don't be afraid to talk about Jesus and the gospel, because when you are doing this, you will **never** be alone. One of these giant angels will be with you!"

Isn't it extraordinary to know we don't have to entertain fear when we witness for God? There is a huge angel standing there with us!

Look around ~ you just might see him!

Angels Calling The People
By Frances

"Look at all those angels standing on the roof of the church!" I exclaimed as we drove from the airport in Fargo, North Dakota, to the First Assembly Of God Church where we were to start a Healing Explosion. "Look! Look! Look! There are angels standing on all four sides of that church! There are angels stationed all the way around the roof and they're all blowing trumpets, calling people in from the North, the South, the East and the West! Isn't that exciting!" The church building has a flat roof and in the spirit I could see all four sides at one time.

The pastor who was driving said, "That really sends goose pimples up and down my spine because just this morning in the prayer meeting we asked God to bring them in from the North, South, East and West for the Healing Explosion! This confirms what we prayed this morning!"

When the time came for the Healing Explosion to start, God's angels had blown those trumpets so clearly that people streamed in from all four directions. For the first time in the history of the city of Fargo, they had a traffic jam! Fargo is not a really big city but so many thousands of people came to the Healing Explosion they had to park their cars in the surrounding cornfields!

When angels get busy on their trumpets ~ watch out ~ things happen!

Angel Touches the Unsaved Man
By Charles

Accepting an invitation to a wedding can bring unexpected surprises! Shortly before it was time for the ceremony to start, a man brought his badly crippled wife into the foyer of the church. She was moaning because she was in such excruciating pain from a bad back problem, and we immediately began to minister healing to her in Jesus' Name!

The wedding was scheduled to start, but the woman

wasn't completely healed. God had put her in traction, and it took about ten minutes for the total healing to manifest. She was so excited she was rejoicing! We couldn't blame her for that, but this delay made the groom extremely nervous. We told him that we knew in our hearts God wanted to finish the miracle first. He agreed, and the lady was then totally healed of months of agonizing pain! The lady got her miracle and the wedding began.

Something very supernatural happened while the minister was conducting the wedding, and I asked him if I could interrupt for a moment. The bride and groom were facing us as we faced the audience. I told the people who had come to share in the blessing of this couple, that it was an unusual wedding because the giant angel whom God had stationed with us was standing directly in back of the bride and groom, facing us. Then he moved to my right, and then back to Frances' side.

At that time, I had never seen this angel nor any of the large angels, but God has given me the ability in the spirit to tell exactly where the angel is and to know his movements.

Frances took the microphone and said, "Charles described him perfectly," (she saw him as plainly as she could see me), and she saw him when he moved to our right and put his hand on the shoulder of the unsaved man sitting there.

That man accepted Jesus that night after the wedding!

Who wouldn't get saved after being touched by an angel!?!

An Angel Confronts a Backslidden Pastor
By Frances

During the worship period of an awesome meeting, as I looked out in the congregation, I saw our angel leaning over a man. Instantly I knew something supernatural was going to happen. I was wrapped up with anticipation, and as soon as we stopped singing, I said to the audience, "Praise the Lord, an angel is here tonight and he is ministering to a man in the audience." Mentioning the approximate area where the angel was, everyone turned around to see if they could catch a glimpse of the angel. Shortly after this, the angel disappeared. Apparently he had done his work and then had vanished!

When the service was over, I heard the most amazing story! The man to whom the angel had ministered was a backslidden pastor! He had left his wife, ran off with his secretary, but apparently an angel brought him into our meeting. Angels have ways that they can urge or prompt you to do something according to God's will and timing. He said the angel ministered to him, encouraging and strengthening him to make a decision to give his heart back to Jesus that night and to return to his wife...and that's just what he did!

"Business" Angels
By Charles

The subject of angels is fascinating to teach in a Bible school. Several years ago I got up early one morning and studied as much as I could about angels since I was teaching on that subject. I said, "God, why can't we 'shift gears' as though it were and see into the angel realm and see their activities?" This was just a thought-prayer and I didn't say anything to Frances about it.

As we passed a small shopping area while driving from our home to the teaching center Frances said, "Charles, do you see all those angels out there today?"

I tried to see them but reluctantly said, "No."

She calmly said, "They must really have a busy day scheduled because they are rushing along carrying something. It looks like a huge briefcase as if they are headed on a mission somewhere." They were just above ground level!

God has blessed her to allow her to see into the spirit realm. She can often see angels as though she is turning on a television set. She sometimes says, "I just back up in the spirit" and really she is saying, "I'll block out my normal thinking and open my heart to see the angels." She said there were hundreds of these "business angels" going to and fro about their work.

Aren't you glad they are out there taking care of your business for you?

Big Jesus
By Charles

A number of years ago Frances developed a horse-shoe shaped tear in her eye and had to have a surgical procedure done which the doctors called a "Cryo." They simply "ironed" the eye back together surgically! It was considered a minor operation but they gave her very strict instructions when she left the hospital. The doctor said, "You cannot travel for at least a week. Your eye must heal completely before you travel. You cannot allow anything to bump against you because you could lose the sight in that eye if you are not extremely careful."

We had already scheduled speaking engagements in San Diego and Fresno, California, which we knew I would have to take alone. We could not cancel this because of our commitment to God to be there.

Before I left, we went into the kitchen and were talking about how we felt about being apart. God joined our hearts together so perfectly when we were married that we can hardly bear being apart even for a short time. I looked into her eye and was shocked to see there was a solid pool of blood! Panic hit our hearts as we remembered what the doctor had told us, so I touched her eyes and we both instantly cried out, "In Jesus' Name!"

We called the emergency ward of the hospital and talked to the doctor on duty that night. He asked if she could still see out of her eye. He instructed her to close the other eye and test it to see if the sight was still there. We were both relieved when we discovered her sight was there! The doctor told us it was most likely a ruptured vessel and would be all right!

That was wonderful to hear, but we still had a lot of concern and trepidation in our hearts about the condition of her eye, remembering that the doctors had said if the eye tore in a complete circle she could be totally blind in that eye.

Regardless of this, we knew we had to fulfill our commitment to God! The next morning, after reluctantly kissing my beloved good-bye, I went to the airport to fly to San Diego for our first three-day engagement, feeling as though I was leaving part of my very own flesh behind.

I prayed and fasted for three days, drawing very close to God. There was nothing on my mind except what I was doing for God and what He was doing for my beloved during our separation. Even that short period of time seemed like an eternity to me.

At the end of the three days I flew to Fresno, California. Frances had healed sufficiently by that time, so the surgeon gave her permission to travel. She met me in Fresno for another three-day crusade, wearing dark glasses.

In our first service, the two of us, the pastor, his wife and the worship team were on the stage during the praise and worship.

Suddenly an amazing miracle happened! There were about two thousand people in the auditorium which was approximately as tall as a three-story building. In the twinkling of an eye, as if someone had suddenly turned on a light switch, I saw two giant columns. They resembled pictures I had seen of Samson in the temple.

As I looked at these columns, there appeared a giant angel in front of each one of them. I looked at them with utter astonishment. They appeared as giant men standing with their feet on the floor with their heads almost touching the three-story-high ceiling. The entire atmosphere was charged with the supernatural energy of God!

Each angel was standing as if in military formation and with a large spear, in military terms "at rest," as if they were guarding something or someone!

As I was looking at both of these giant angels, suddenly my spirit was taken to the back of the auditorium and there was a whole group of angels who looked as though they were active in some other way. I didn't understand what they were doing but they were clearly visible.

Then as my spirit—mind began to seemingly "float" over the auditorium, my attention became riveted on the very center—front aisle of the civic center.

As I continued watching that scene, I saw a third great, giant man with His feet on the floor and His head almost touching the ceiling. **And there stood Jesus!** What an awesome feeling it was to behold Jesus! My heart stood still!

I couldn't even think of angels any more because of the glory of God on our Lord Jesus! As I watched this spectacular vision, the spirits of each of those approximately two thousand people suddenly left their bodies like vapors and went right into the body of Jesus and disappeared!

When they had totally disappeared into Jesus, the scene again changed and the only way I can describe it is to say that Jesus became as big as the universe. No longer was He contained in the building where we were worshiping, He was out of the limits of space! As I watched this huge mighty Jesus, the powerful Son of God, this vision suddenly changed dimension when Jesus, as big as the universe, became small enough to go into each of the two thousand people in the auditorium! Then He disappeared!

What a revelation! It was almost too overwhelming to comprehend, but as I continued to watch, God spoke. "When you are completely in Jesus, then Jesus will be completely in you."

The apostle Paul wrote, Colossians 1:27, *Christ in you the hope of glory.*

God was showing me very clearly that "Christ in you is the hope of glory" and also that Jesus lives in and through each of His believers.

This is a never-to-be-forgotten miracle-vision of our Lord Jesus Christ and the angels. It changed my life!

Escorted To Heaven By Angels
By Charles

In 1968 God had drawn me like a magnet into a very close walk with Jesus. My wife was dying and ultimately died of cancer and I was spending huge amounts of time in the Bible just loving God and Jesus. My only desire was to love them more and more and to have a more intimate relationship with them. I spent hundreds of hours, perhaps even thousands, in the Bible during which time stories about angels didn't necessarily impress me that much because that was not what I was focusing on at that time!

One thing that vividly impressed me, though, was

when a Christian dies angels escort them to heaven!
They can also escort you to places in the natural while
you are alive.

Finally the beggar died and was carried by the
angels to be with Abraham in the place of the
righteous dead (Luke 16:22 TLB).

When my wife died, the head nurse was checking
her pulse and suddenly said, "She's gone." I replied,
"Yes, I know." I actually saw her spirit, almost like a
vapor, leave her body and zoom up toward heaven. I
knew instantly she had died, but believe, just like the
beggar in Luke 16:22, that angels came and took her
soul and spirit to heaven. That night God again blessed
me by letting me see her in a vision, in heaven, singing
in a choir.

In 1968, while this was happening in my life, I was
lying on a cot in the hospital room looking up to God
and praising Him. Earlier that night God had audibly
spoken to me through my hearing mechanism. That
was a phenomenal experience and I could hardly comprehend that the Almighty God would speak to an ordinary person in a huge city like Houston, Texas. Because
He audibly spoke to me, I was lying on the bed looking
up to God and thanking Him and praising Him for
letting me have that remarkable experience. I was awed
by this. I said, "God, people in the Bible have heard
you speak and have talked to you and we know you
always listen."

While I was lying there, suddenly I looked up above

me and saw a body suspended in air about eighteen inches above my physical body. As I began looking at this and pondering about it, I could see through this body like looking through a thin fog or cloud but I could clearly see this body! It was the same size as me, it was the same shape as me and when I looked at the face, it was my face!

As I was watching this phenomenal scene I said, "God, you have taken my spirit out of my wide awake healthy body and allowed me to see it!"

A great prayer warrior had said earlier that night, "I am going to lift you up in the light of God in prayer." She was actually praying for my wife but she spoke that to me and it sounded peculiar that she would be praying for me, but she did. She said, "I am going into my bedroom and pray and I'm going to lift you up into the light of God." I thought that was simply an expression ~ I didn't realize it was God moving in a special way that particular night.

I saw a vision of this lady whom I had never seen, with her hands under my back lifting me up. When I got as high as her arms would reach, suddenly an energy began to flow through my body from my feet up to my head like repeated waves of the sea. I was aware of this tremendous surge of the power of God, and that I was ascending into the air. I began to move upward, first slowly like a rocket taking off and then suddenly I was going at a very, very rapid speed. I didn't feel any resistance from gravity or any other thing but I could tell I was moving extremely fast through space.

While I was watching this, suddenly my "thinker"

moved from my head into that other body. The thinking never changed from the way I was thinking while I
was in this human body but it continued in a normal
way as I was thinking to God, which I often do.

I didn't realize it at the time, but now I am quite
aware that the Bible says in Hebrews 4:12 (KJV):

For the word of God is quick, and powerful, and
sharper than any two-edged sword, piercing even
to the dividing asunder of soul and spirit...

Later I realized what God was doing. He had taken
my spirit out of my wide awake healthy body and then
took my soul out to join my spirit and I began to move
upward at this rapid rate. I didn't see anything as I was
going, but it was as though I was able to see, yet not see.
It seemed like six or seven seconds passed until suddenly my spirit and soul stopped and as I looked, the
whole sky, which is normally blue or cloudy, was absolutely the most beautiful golden sky I had ever seen. It
was far more pure than any gold that I had ever looked
at on earth.

I only stayed in the glory of the light of God as far as
my mind comprehended another six or seven seconds
when suddenly my body began to descend. It didn't fall
but was lowered by an unseen force, just like when I
went up, and was moving rapidly back down to earth.
When I got just a little above my earthly body it was like
I hit an air pocket and my spirit and soul entered back
into my physical body and I was aware that I was back
to my normal human self. My mind continued to think
just as it always had and then I began to realize God had

taken me on a journey to heaven and allowed me to see all of this supernatural experience, held in the marvelous light of God!

I had been escorted on a round trip journey to heaven!

When I understood that angels have the capability of escorting your soul and spirit, I realized that these were angels who escorted my soul and spirit up into the portals of heaven, into the light of God!

CHAPTER 10

Entertaining Angels Unaware

By Frances

Do not forget to entertain strangers, for by so doing some have unwittingly entertained angels (Hebrews 13:2).

A heavenly angelic encounter can redirect your entire life and change your plans forever!

One such meeting, which happened to me, has affected Charles' and my life and possibly the lives of the entire world! Surprisingly, it occurred over a luncheon table in a very small town in Missouri.

Several of our special friends had flown in to minister with us in a series of meetings. Our planes had all arrived at an early hour, so we were thrilled to be able to have lunch together. It was a typical small town restaurant. Good home–cooked food but not a lot of atmosphere! There were ten or twelve of us at the table, and the excitement was at a very high pitch as we were all sharing the miracles God had been doing in our lives. We were anticipating all kinds of Holy Spirit happenings in the upcoming meetings.

We had been seated for just a few moments when a man completely unknown to me walked up to the table and said, "May I join you?" I answered, "Yes," because he spoke directly to me. He then sat down at the end of our table. Charles was sitting next to me at the side of the table and the stranger sat at the end of the table next to Charles. I assumed he was a friend of the pastor who was sitting directly across from me.

Just for a moment it struck me as being a little peculiar that the stranger began to talk to *me*. He didn't say, "Hello," or even speak to any of the others at the table. He didn't even indicate that he was aware of anyone else being at the table, including Charles, but focused his attention solely on me.

To help you better understand what occurred next, I want to explain that I was one of those Jesus fanatics from the word "go!" The day I got saved, I had a violent never-to-be-forgotten encounter with the Lord Jesus Christ! When I say "violent," I don't mean I cried or rolled on the floor or anything as dramatic as that, but when I met Him it was a dynamic personal encounter that impacted my life forever and ever and ever! I had walked into church with the smell of cigarettes on my breath and alcohol in my body, but with a determination in my heart that morning that I was not going to leave that church until I knew that I knew, that I *knew,* that I *knew* that Jesus Christ was actually living in my heart!

I had a most unusual encounter with God in a hospital room several months earlier when God's finger, dipped in the brilliant red blood of Jesus, wrote five words in my Bible which are emblazoned on my heart even today: "Frances Gardner (that was my name then), I love you!" Those five precious, never-to-be-forgotten words changed my life forever and ever! But it was about nine months later that I made a momentous decision before I went to church that I was not going to walk out of that church until I knew beyond a shadow of a doubt that Jesus Christ, the Son of the living God, was actually living in my heart!

When that dramatic moment came and I knew Jesus had taken up residence in my heart, I experienced an instantaneous changeover from a wild sinner to a saint of God! In the depths of my heart, somehow I knew that everything I had ever done had been forgiven by God and buried in the deepest sea never to be remembered again! I was totally set free at the ripe old age of forty-nine!

I couldn't wait to get out of the church because there was such a compelling force burning within me from the split second when I asked God to forgive my sins and Jesus to come into my heart, that drove me to want to tell everybody I saw about the saving grace of the Lord Jesus Christ!

I stopped at every store that was open! People thought I had lost my mind because all I wanted to do was talk about Jesus! *I had lost my mind ~ now I possessed the mind of Christ!* My only desire was to bring everyone I knew into the kingdom of God. I walked out of church that day and said, "God, I've got to win the whole world to Jesus because nobody is talking about Him!"

Little did I know that some day Charles and I would be called by God to coordinate a World Evangelistic Census where, as Jesus said, the gospel will be preached to every creature.

The reason I felt this way and burned with such an intensity in my whole being to share the gospel of salvation was because no one had ever shared the gospel with me until I was forty–eight years of age!

I had gone to church all my life. I had done all the "things" people involved in "churchianity" do, but there had never been that personal confrontation with Jesus. Up until that time, no one had ever asked me if I had ever met Jesus, if I knew Jesus, or whether I was saved.

However, there was a day when I walked up on the porch of the church where I eventually got saved, that a girl said to me, "Hi, Frances! When did you get *saved?*"

There was something about that word "*saved*" that stuck a knife right into the innermost depths of my heart. I didn't even know what it meant. So I asked, "Saved from what?" All I remember is that word *saved* pierced and penetrated the core of my very being, and unknown to me, convicted me.

So when I knew that I knew that *I was saved,* I took off determined that the whole world was going to get saved. I didn't care what I had to do to accomplish this impossible task but I knew somehow or other that I had to do it!

As a result of this drive within me, which has never ceased or even cooled down, I have been known as a soulwinner wherever I go. My second book, *"Go, Man, Go!"* was strictly about witnessing and was written at a time when I didn't really even know how to witness, but I was still leading a lot of people to Jesus.

Since then, my zeal for winning souls has only increased! Because of this consuming drive, I believe God planned a very special encounter for me in that little Missouri restaurant.

The stranger who sat at our table was very interesting in that he was dressed in a nondescript way. There was nothing outstanding about his clothing that I could remember, and I vaguely remembered his facial characteristics later. The one thing I do recall quite clearly, though, was the compelling personality he had! When he began to talk to me, I could not hear or listen to anyone else! There was a supernatural drawing to this individual whom I had never met before.

Our conversation started in a very interesting manner. He said, "Frances, I know about your reputation for being a tremendous soulwinner and I want to show you a new way to win people to Jesus."

Although I did not recognize this man, I assumed he was a pastor or a friend of the pastor, so I responded, "Tell me!" I'm always interested in whatever will bring people into the kingdom of God, whether it's an altar call, a one-to-one basis, or however it is, so my attention was riveted to what he was going to share.

His answer, however, was not exactly what I had expected at all because he said, "Do you see that waitress over there?"

I answered, "Yes."

He said, "She's going to come over here and the very first thing she's going to say is, 'What would you like to drink?'"

That's a well–known approach, because that's the first thing every waitress or waiter asks when you sit down at a table in a restaurant. They never ask first for your food order; they always ask for your drink order first.

This man obviously knew she was going to be like every other waitress in every other restaurant and he said, "When she says that to me, I'm going to answer, 'Water.' Then I'm going to ask, 'Now may I ask you a question?' Her answer will be, 'Yes.'

"I will say to her, 'Do you know there are two kinds of beautiful waitresses in this restaurant?'

"She is going to reply, 'Really?'

"Then I'm going to say, 'Yes, those who are saved and those who are about to be. Which one are you?'"

Without one second of time passing, something literally exploded on the inside of me! From the minute the stranger started to talk, I never took my eyes off him, nor could I hear the other conversations going on at our table. It was sort of a situation of, "Just you and me, brother, and I don't even know who you are!" When he said, "Those who are saved and those who are about to be," something happened within me that I absolutely cannot explain.

Without any question or doubt in my mind, without even trying it the first time, I saw that this was a "win/ win" situation where there was no way you could lose. If the person was already saved, you would say, "Praise the Lord! That makes you my brother (or sister)!" and if they were not saved, you've given them no other choice than to give you the answer you want, which is, "I'm about to be!"

There are all different kinds of people in the world, and I think it's wonderful that God didn't make us little carbon copies of one another. He made each and every one of us individual, distinct and different in our approach to life. I happen to be one of those who is a real "eager beaver." I'm not the type who says, "Well, let me see you do it and then let me see you do it fifty more times, *then* maybe I'll have the courage to try it."

The minute I hear something that strikes me as being exciting or outstanding, I want to try it right away! Because this had so touched my heart, so electrified me, I couldn't wait to get started! As soon as he paused, I exclaimed, "Let me do it! Let me do it! Let me do it!" I didn't even want to wait to see him do it because something in my spirit had so leaped within me that I knew instantly this was an incredibly effective way to win people to Jesus. Certainly it was the simplest, easiest way I had ever heard or seen.

He very softly said, "Okay."

When the waitress came up to me and asked what I

wanted to drink, I ordered water and then said, "May I ask you a question?"

She said, "Yes."

I said, "Do you know there are two kinds of beautiful waitresses in this restaurant?" Please note that I said exactly word—for—word what the man had said. I later understood why I did that.

The waitress said, "Really?" (just like he said she would!)

Then I said, "Yes! Those who are saved and those who are about to be. Which one are you?"

Without any instruction from the man at the table, I looked directly at the waitress, never taking my eyes off her, and put on my very best smile, because somehow or other I knew it was going to work even though I wasn't really prepared for what happened!

The Holy Spirit fell in a way that words cannot describe. It was as if the waitress and I were enveloped in a special supernatural sack, where everyone else was excluded except the two of us. The presence and power of God was incredible.

I did not say another word. I just waited until she answered and her answer was certainly a shock to me!

She immediately burst into tears, "Boo-hoo! Boo-hoo! Boo-hoo!" crying so loud she could be heard throughout the entire restaurant. Then she stopped and immediately said, "I'm about to be!"

I guess I hadn't thought far enough ahead because all I wanted to do was to try this new method of soul-winning. I was really prepared for an answer but I certainly wasn't prepared for such a spontaneous, emotional reply as this. But, praise the Lord, we possess the mind of Christ and He's always there to tell us what to do in any situation!

I grabbed the waitress's hand so she couldn't get away from me and immediately said, "Repeat this after me: Father, forgive my sins." Without questioning me at all, she said, "Father, forgive my sins."

Then I continued, "Jesus, come into my heart and save me."

She repeated, "Jesus, come into my heart and save me."

I said, "Thank You, Jesus for saving me!"

She replied, "Thank You, Jesus for saving me!"

Then I instantly asked her the most important question of all, "Where is Jesus right now?" She burst into tears again and said, "In my heart!"

She gave the answer which so many people who have gone to church for many, many years do not understand, and that is the principle of what Paul preached, *"Christ in you, the hope of glory"* (Colossians 1:27).

Her answer was so fast that there was absolutely no question in her mind whatsoever that Jesus Christ had come to live in her heart and she was saved! She began crying so hard that she had to go back to the kitchen where she cried for ten more minutes before she returned to take our order!

As soon as this had happened, the man who taught me this said, "I have another appointment and need to go now. Would you mind if I left?"

I said, "No, but thank you so much for sharing this with me because I think it's tremendous!"

I remember that as I watched him get up and walk toward the door of the restaurant, I had the most unusual feeling when he left my presence, as though he was not an ordinary person. Wondering whether he was a famous evangelist or perhaps a pastor with a really special anointing, I turned to the pastor sitting across the table from me and asked, "Who was that man?"

The pastor answered, "What man?"

I said, "The man I was just talking to at the end of the table."

He replied, "I didn't see anybody."

I said, "The man who told me how to do 'There Are Two Kinds of...'"

The pastor answered, "I didn't hear anybody. I thought that was your idea."

"No," I said, "it wasn't my idea at all. That man told me exactly what to do."

Again he replied, "I didn't see anybody!"

I turned to Charles, who was sitting right next to me, *between* the man I'd talked to and me and asked, "Charles, do you know that man?"

Again I heard the words, "What man? I didn't see anybody."

"The man I was talking to." By this time I was really puzzled.

Charles answered, "I didn't hear anybody."

I turned to the people at the other end of the table because at this point I was really astonished and amazed.

I asked, "Do any of you know who that man was who told me how to do, 'There Are Two Kinds of...'?" Of all the people at the table, only two others thought they saw someone but no one heard him speaking except me.

I didn't really think too much about this except that this encounter had so turned me on that I got up from the table and said, "I have to find the rest of the waitresses, the cashier, the cooks, let me get the busboys! This is the easiest and most awesome way to win people to Jesus I've ever seen!" I just exploded right there in the restaurant.

They had heard me speak to the first waitress and they all thought it was an absolutely wonderful idea, so all of us started using this method immediately with awesome results.

We collectively decided, because of the success of this simple little soul-winning tool, to eat at different restaurants the entire time we were there so that we could get all of the waiters and waitresses in town saved! We shared it in the church that night and told them to go out and do the same thing and the results were incredible.

The telephone lines were really busy for the next few weeks because all of us who had sat at that especially anointed luncheon table were saying, "There are two kinds of..." to everybody we met, and everyone was having exactly the same wonderful success.

Every time they called, I would say again, "Are you sure you don't know who that man was?" And their answer, of course, was always the same. We didn't see him or the two that thought they saw him said they had absolutely no idea who he was.

Charles started in our grocery store. We have a big supermarket very close to where we live and where there are a lot of bag boys. He would have them carry the groceries out to the car and on the way out he would say, "Do you know there are two kinds of executive bag boys?" We always try to put a complimentary adjective in there because that really gets their attention!

We have been thrilled to discover that about ninety-five of the possibly one hundred bag boys who were working in the store at that time gave the same response. "Really?"

Then Charles would tell them and they would say, "Well, I'm the one who is about to be." We had such an exciting time that we got to the point where we wouldn't even carry a quart of milk out without a bag boy because that was just one more opportunity to win a soul to Jesus.

A lady came into our office recently and said, "Something just happened at a grocery store that I have got to share with you because it must be the store where Charles and Frances Hunter shop." She continued, "As I was checking out, the bag boy was singing and looked like the happiest person in the world. I said to him, 'You are really happy.'

"He answered, 'Yes! Some "old man" came in here a week ago and I got saved and I've been happy ever since!'"

This really impressed the lady, but she was even more

impressed when a young man two counters down said, "Did that 'old man' get you too? He got me about a month ago and it changed my life when I got saved!"

Charles didn't mind being called "an old man" when it brings someone into the kingdom of God.

We have shared this exciting method around the United States and some people have really caught the vision of what the man said. Some friends of ours have done an incredible job, and one of my favorite stories of theirs has a real element of surprise!

A telephone call can be a very interesting opportunity. This friend of ours answered the telephone and obviously the person calling didn't recognize her voice. He said, "I'm sorry. I must have dialed the wrong telephone number."

She quickly answered, "No, you got the right number but there are two kinds of people who *think* they dialed the wrong number; those who are saved and those who are about to be ~ which are you?"

"I guess I'm about to be because nobody ever asked me that question before," the man replied. He prayed with her asking Jesus to come into his heart and was very grateful. He profoundly thanked her over and over again for asking him that "two kinds" of question.

We challenge you to take advantage of every opportunity (every person) who comes before you! Jesus said, "*Go into all the world and preach the gospel to every creature,*" and He also said to start in Jerusalem, your home town.

As we were writing this book we went to have a

quick dinner at a local fast-food place. We were waiting for our order when a little four-year-old girl walked up to our table and asked, "Do you know Jesus?"

"Yes," I replied with a smile, "Do you know Him?"
She said, "Yes."
I asked, "Do you love Him like I do?"
And she replied, "Yes, I love Him very much."

While this conversation was going on, a young lady came up to Charles and said, "I am the waitress here, so if there is anything you need after you pick up your order, I'll be very glad to get it for you." She added, "Is there anything I can do for you right now?"

Charles said, "Yes. You can answer this question. Do you know there are two kinds of beautiful waitresses in this restaurant? Those who are saved and those who are about to be, which are you?" There was no hesitation whatsoever. She simply said, "I'm about to be," so she prayed the sinner's prayer.

The lady at the next table overheard us and said, "I couldn't help but hear that Name. I want to talk to you because you must have been leading that lady to Jesus." She had no more than gotten these words out of her mouth when this same waitress came back with a young man.

She said, "Would you please give him what you gave me because he needs it, too." So Charles asked the young man the question and he accepted Jesus as his Savior and Lord.

By this time, the conversation on our side of the restaurant was about Jesus, so we were really having an exciting time although we hardly had the opportunity to eat any of our dinner (who cares?).

Soon the same waitress came back again. "I've got another one for you. Would you give to him what you gave to me because he really needs it. He stole my tip yesterday!"

The thing that excited us so much was the fact that when that one girl got the message she became an instant disciple! When we left she said, "Please come back to dinner again real soon because there's a lot of them in here that I would like to bring over to you!"

If we could just get one person like that at each of our churches, wouldn't it be exciting...especially if that one person was YOU!

Because Charles likes to use the name of Jesus (which is wonderful) he started saying, "Those who have accepted Jesus and those who are about to." This worked, but not nearly as well as when we said, "Those who are saved and those who are about to be." And yet, there is so much power in the name of Jesus that Charles said, "I really think that gives it more credibility ~ when you say the name of Jesus." He continued for a time saying it that way, and while he led many people to Jesus, he did not have the success he could have had and should have had.

We were discussing this with a pastor in the state of Colorado, and I was telling him about the unusual characteristics of the man who told me about "There are two kinds of..." and the sensation I had when he was talking to me. I said that I really wished I could find out who he was so I could thank him.

I also mentioned to the pastor about Charles changing it to, "Those who have accepted Jesus..." and my saying, "Those who are saved..." He looked at me and said words that sent mountain-size shivers up and down my spine, "Did it ever dawn on you that it was an angel bringing you God's special end-time revival message? That's the reason it has been so successful because it *came straight from God!*" He continued, "I wouldn't change one word the *angel* said!"

The realization of the truth of what he had said was like a bombshell exploding! I looked at Charles and exclaimed, "**IT WAS AN ANGEL!**"

Suddenly I understood why only two *thought* they saw the man and why no one heard him except me. It was an angelic messenger God had sent directly to me to bring the end–time revival message!

We all started saying, "Those who are saved and those who are about to be..." and discovered without a doubt, it is the most incredible way in the world to lead people to Jesus. No wonder ~ it was sent by God and personally delivered by an angel!

Little did we realize that the angelic visitation we received on an ordinary day in a little restaurant in southeast Missouri would change not only our lives and our way of witnessing but would change the world as well!

We immediately changed all of our World Evangelistic Census packets to use the method brought by an angel. To date over 125 million documented salvations have been reported. That number is daily mounting as people all over the world are excitedly knocking on doors and saying, "Do you know there are two kinds of people..."

"Old" birthdays can be the most exciting thing in the world!

The righteous shall flourish like a palm tree, He shall grow like a cedar in Lebanon. Those who are planted in the house of the Lord shall flourish in the courts of our God. They shall still bear fruit in old age; they shall be fresh and flourishing (Psalm 92:12-14).

Some birthdays are much more unusual than others! My eighty-second birthday was one of those! I wanted something special for my birthday, so I asked God to give me **30 million souls!**

We had seen the World Evangelistic Census go forward in such tremendous leaps and bounds, so when 25 million souls had been won to Jesus world-wide by the first of April, 1998, I decided that surely we could get 30 million by the beginning of May!

Reports came in every day and the totals climbed and climbed and climbed. We had prayed and prayed, and the salvations really came in, but the night before my birthday, we were still 145,643 short of the 30 million! We called everyone we knew and asked them to really pray that somehow or another God would supernaturally send in the salvations needed for my birthday.

Then we asked God to send angels out to bring in the reports so that we would have it on my birthday!

Angels can move quickly so we knew they could do it in a short period of time!

At bedtime we were still short of the 30 million, but God answers prayers in the most incredible ways! Thank God for faxes and e-mails in the world today! At 10:30 PM we were abruptly awakened when we received a fax from the coordinator in the Philippines with a partial report from the eastern side of Region 6 showing 173,324 new souls born into the kingdom of God. God not only gave us 30 million, He gave us exceedingly, abundantly above all that we could ask or think! What rejoicing there was in our house that night!

Thank You, Father, that angels are special messengers who bring good reports!

CHAPTER 11

End-Time Dreams, Visions And Angelic Visitations

By Frances

An angelic encounter can have eternal effects! Every time I think about the angel at a luncheon table in Missouri and what has happened as a result of that visitation, my heart leaps with excitement!

Many other things have been tied into that angelic visit, one of which was an end-time dream and vision.

Charles and I had gone to Terre Haute, Indiana, for a meeting over the Memorial Day weekend. We had arrived in the late part of the afternoon and, having had a no-food flight, we decided to have a bite to eat before we went to bed.

Once seated in the hotel dining room, we examined the menu and noticed in the list of side dishes something that caught my fancy. It simply said, "Mashed potatoes with whole roasted garlic cloves." That really grabbed my attention because I had never seen that on a menu before. Since both of us love garlic (but we can't eat it too often because of speaking dates!) we decided that, since it was Saturday night and we didn't have any meetings until Sunday morning, it would be okay to eat it. So I ordered mashed potatoes with whole garlic cloves. You might ask, "How spiritual is garlic?"

The Jewish people ate leeks and garlic in Old Testament times, so I guess it's really a good idea. When you discover what happened as a result of our potent meal, you might want to try some mashed potatoes and roasted garlic cloves, too!

Shortly after eating, we went to bed because we wanted to be sure we were totally refreshed for Sunday morning. Sleep came over us very quickly and during the night I had a dream, a very unusual dream!

Usually, when I dream, the dreams don't make sense. Since they don't make sense while I'm dreaming them, I'm never very concerned about the dreams which I have. This particular night, though, I had a dream which will stay with me as long as I live and it was not a garlic dream. It was a godly message.

The dream started with Charles and I entering our office one morning. This particular day we came in early, about the same time that our staff was arriving, because we had a tremendous work load staring us in the face that day. When we walked through the door I saw and heard an unusual thing!

All the telephones rang and the lines lit up at the same time! In actuality there are six telephone lines coming into our office, but in this dream we had increased them to ten lines and all of them were lit up.

We have only eight other employees in the office and the two of us make ten, so we knew when we saw the ten lines lit up that we both had to answer a telephone. Charles ran very quickly down to his office; I turned and went into mine and picked up the telephone and got the shock of my life!

The man on the telephone said, "We just ended an evangelistic census in the country of _____, (some African nation with which I was not familiar,) and 794,622 people were saved!" I thought, Wow! This is really exciting! I didn't even know we had anyone working in that nation! When people call in, we don't just take down the figures, we confirm them by calling them back. There are some people who would like to throw the World Evangelistic Census off by reporting false figures. I asked the gentleman for his telephone number and asked him for a little more information. He was so excited because when he first heard about the census he said he wasn't really too interested because he didn't think such a simple plan would work. Then, he said the more he thought about it, the more he talked to God about it, and the more he realized that this was really God's end-time message, the more excited he became, particularly since the way to win people to Jesus was brought by an angel directly from the throne room of God. We had a little conversation, and the entire time I was on the phone with him, I observed that all the other phone lines continued to stay lit. As soon as one light went out, it would immediately turn red again by another call coming in.

When I finished the conversation, I was so excited I

could hardly wait to tell Charles! I thought, Wow! This is really an awesome thing when you get a telephone call from a country we weren't even aware was involved in the census! But I didn't even get my telephone hung up before it rang again. In my dream, I looked over toward my secretary's room and saw her foot stick out the door like she was going to walk into my office but then it disappeared when her phone rang.

This kept up all day long. All the telephone lines continued to stay lit up. None of us could have made a call out because there were no lines available. We wouldn't even have had time to make any calls because apparently everybody was on the telephone the entire time. Every time my secretary would start to come in to tell me something, her phone would ring again and she would have to go back in and answer it.

God's Word says,

"Not by might nor by power, but by My Spirit,"
and His Spirit is moving all over the earth. If we want to be walking in the spirit, we have to move when God's Spirit moves. So we stayed by the phones!

As the dream continued, I never got up from my desk, and an amazing thing began to occur. The office was, of course, in a state of confusion because everybody was talking on the telephone and nobody got to share with anyone else what was going on.

Suddenly I heard a tremendous roar outside the office. Our office is in the country, and we have a little road that runs in front of it where there is not a lot of traffic. But at that moment I heard an unbelievable roar

~ and that's exactly what it was! ~ a roar, a tremendously loud sound coming down the street. It was coming closer and closer. Strangely, I knew that the sound was not made by automobiles or trucks because it wasn't coming that fast but it was advancing as though people were marching or walking.

I could not get up from my desk to go see what it was because I was on the telephone, and yet I continued to hear this roar which kept escalating in volume. Before I even had time to consider what it was, the front door of our office burst open and in came what seemed like thousands of people! We have both an office and a warehouse where we store our books, and the funny thing is that the entire building, including the warehouse, was suddenly and completely filled with people.

There were thousands of faces, all shouting and yelling! Each of them had their hands full of little white slips of paper which I instantly recognized as being the forms that we give out all over the world for people to sign when they get saved. All the offices filled up rapidly with people and suddenly, because there was no more room to stand in the offices, people began climbing up on the desks! In the spirit, even though I was sitting in my own office, I could see into the warehouse and all the other offices and exactly the same thing was happening. Before I'd hardly turned around there were eight or ten people standing on my desk! That's a lot of people!

They were all shoving pieces of paper at me and yelling and shouting, but I could tell that they were not an angry mob but were people who were excited! They were so excited about what was happening that they could hardly contain themselves.

They utterly invaded our office! When the office got so jammed that no one else could even attempt to squeeze in, I happened to look out through one of the windows in my office and saw crowds of people standing outside the building all the way around. They were standing on one another's shoulders trying to see into my window, waving little pieces of paper outside the window. The little pieces of paper were all the slips telling the number of salvations from various nations.

I can't ever remember going through a day like that in my entire life! All I know is that it was the most exciting day I'd ever had, and even though I didn't get to talk to Charles or any of our office staff before the day was done, I knew in my spirit that everything that was happening was of God and was wonderful and exciting.

When the day finally ended and the people suddenly disappeared, all of our employees ran into my office. They were all talking at one time, each one saying exactly the same thing about how many people had called. There was no way that anyone had an opportunity to add up the totals of the salvations, but everyone said the only phone calls they took all day long were telling us about salvations. Some of these were from nations we didn't even know existed, so we had to get the people to spell the name of their country! The peculiar thing is that all the people who called, even though they were from foreign nations, all managed to speak English and communicate with us so we got all their totals down.

When I awoke from the dream I could hardly contain myself because it was so exciting. It had been so real that, even as I write this, I can still see the faces of the people who were standing on my desk. Then we found out later that everybody in every office had people standing on their desks too, because there wasn't room to stand anywhere else! The results were exactly the same from everybody. Everyone was yelling and saying, "Oh, Frances! Look what I've got! Look what I've got!" They were all showing me nothing but Evangelistic Census reports.

I immediately began sharing with Charles and telling him about what had happened in my dream. We both decided that this was a visitation of the Holy Spirit in a dream or possibly through an angel. Whatever His method of speaking to us, we believed God was saying, "Get ready for an explosion in the World Evangelistic Census because this is what I'm going to do. Then when it's over, Jesus will be back and all will be ended!"

I could hardly wait to call our office on Monday morning to tell our staff about the dream. In our spirits we both knew that this was God preparing us to get ready because He is going to do an outstanding work in the Evangelistic Census.

When I called the office on Monday morning, the phone was answered by our graphics man, who has been with us for more than thirteen years. Normally he doesn't answer the telephone, but this particular morning, because this was God's plan, he answered. The first thing he said was not, "How did the meeting go yesterday?" or anything like he would normally ask. He simply said, "Frances, would you like to hear a dream I had Saturday night?"

This, of course, shocked me since I'd had such an unusual dream on Saturday night. I first responded, "Wait until you hear the dream I had!" But then I politely replied, "Tell me yours first!"

He was really excited as he said, "You know I don't dream very often." He had my attention because the same thing is true of me, and in all the years he's worked for us, I've never heard him talk about any dream he's had. He went on, "I had the most unusual dream Saturday night. I dreamed we moved our offices into a sixty story office building, and our offices were on the top floor. I had to go down to the first floor to take some work, so I got on the elevator and pushed the button for the first floor. The elevator started to move but suddenly it stopped at the fifty-ninth floor.

"The doors opened and I never saw anything like it in my life! The entire fifty-ninth floor of the building was filled with thousands of people and they were all waving these little slips of paper and shoving them at me because they contained the names of people who had accepted Jesus!" He continued, "I never saw so many people before and never saw so many handfuls of these WEC forms as I saw. The people were frantically waving them at me but there was no way I could take them all! I thought, 'What if all these people try to get on the elevator? We'll drop like a stone!' Somehow the people were prevented from getting on the elevator. I pushed the button again and the doors closed, but we stopped at the fifty-eighth floor this time! When the elevator doors opened, it was exactly the same as on the fifty-ninth floor!

"When the elevator doors opened, I saw that the whole floor was full of people jammed together as tightly as possible, waving thousands of little pieces of paper showing the number of people who had been saved in the various countries." He said, "Somehow the people were stopped from getting on the elevator by an invisible force, but I never saw so much excitement and yelling and carrying on!

"I pressed the button again, still trying to get to the first floor. The doors closed and when they opened again we were on the fifty-seventh floor! It was exactly the same as the previous floors! From there, the elevator stopped at every floor from the top all the way to the first floor and it was exactly the same every time the elevator doors slid open."

When I told him what I had dreamed, he responded that God had said to him, "We need to prepare to enlarge in order to take care of all the salvations that are coming in through the World Evangelistic Census!"

If you will think back on both of these dreams, you will realize that they are both exactly the same thing, just given in a different manner!

I shared this at one of the church services and the pastor came running up and said:

"In 1984, in Louisiana, God awakened me in the middle of a Wednesday night about 11:30 and while everyone was in bed He spoke to me audibly. At first I was a little frightened. I thought I was going crazy. I looked in the kitchen to see if somebody was playing a game with me and there was nobody there. My sons were in bed. My wife was in bed.

"Again the voice came and said, 'Get on the floor, I want to talk to you.' The Lord spoke to me audibly for some time. That happened two nights in a row. The third night He did the same thing, and then He gave me a vision. I had never had a vision before or since like this. I have had heart visions. I have had dreams that I knew were from the Lord. I shook my head, opened my eyes, tried to get rid of it but couldn't. He wanted to show me something.

"The second night I think I left my body, the best I can tell. I went above the earth and was standing in space 'outside of time' looking down at the earth. There was no time involved. This was the first time I had been 'outside of time.' I could feel the Lord standing close to me, but I never turned to look at Him. I could feel Him there as He talked to me.

"I would ask Him questions and He would answer. He showed me a wave that billowed up at a certain point of the earth. Picture looking at the earth. It billowed up and then it started to move. On the front side of that wave there was a cutting edge where great and mighty things take place. On the back side there were millions of people getting saved.

"This wave which I called the wave of glory, went around the entire world and He told me to tell everybody about it.

"I was riding in the front of that wave. I saw people getting legs who didn't have legs, hands on people who didn't have hands, crippled bodies straighten up and all kinds of incredible healings. People were preaching in bar rooms, bowling alleys, people getting saved on the sidewalks, miracles were happening.

"The third night God called me again. I got on my face. Same thing. Same situation only this time He took me behind the wave. On the back edge of the wave I saw boats lined up. It would take at least three hours to tell you the whole vision. That glory wave left a huge lake. Thousands of boats were floating on that lake. These boats were lined up nose to nose, side by side all the way around the earth. There was no place where there wasn't a boat. They were everywhere. The people in boats were grabbing folks.

"These people were floundering in the water and that was His glory! Some were drowning in it because they refused help. People in the boats were reaching and grabbing them by the hand, by the hair, by the face, by anything they could get a hold of, pulling and throwing them in the boats, kids, moms, dads, teenagers, just throwing them in. These boats were full and the people weren't sitting orderly. You could see elbows, legs, bottoms, heads!

"I was serious as I could be when I said, 'Lord, those boats are going to sink.' That was my first thought when I saw how full they were. He said, 'Son, those boats don't sink.' When you think they are full enough, there is always room for more. You just keep on bringing the people in!"

As this wave went around the earth, the farther it got the faster it got! When the wave of glory hit where it started, a huge splash went into the air. As that gigantic water spout went into the air, Jesus appeared, and that was the end!

Think about these three supernatural visitations. We believe they are signals from the throne of God that the days are here for which we have eagerly and earnestly longed and of which the Bible says the saints in heaven are envious! We believe the incredible momentum of the census is a gigantic portion of that wave which will be the final END TIME HARVEST!

Part Two

Every Life Needs An Anchor Point

In every life we need to have an "anchor point." A situation, an experience, a special word from God or something of that nature to which we can always go back and look and it will bring our faith to the point where it should be. Many times an angel is involved in the anchor point. We often heard our beloved Pastor John Osteen say, "You could beat me with a baseball bat until I was nothing but a greasy spot, but you could not change my mind about what happened to me on the way home from the Isis Theater one night." That was an anchor point in his life.

I have been blessed with two outstanding anchor points, both of which are mentioned in this book. The first time was when I saw the finger of God dipped into the crimson blood of Jesus, write five words on the pages of my Bible. When He wrote "Frances Gardner" (that was my name then) "I Love You," that is something that you can never take away from me! Regardless of whatever circumstances might come in life there is the knowledge that God said, "I love you."

The second time was told in the first chapter of this book where God spoke telling me He had sent a special warrior angel to protect me from the firey darts of the devil until Jesus Christ comes back again! Those kinds of an-chor points in your life are something that you can hook your Christian anchor to and know that it will always hold.

These anchor points can be many different types of situations. In Charles' life it was when he was taken up to the portals of heaven as told also in this book. You could not take that away from him regardless of how you tried, because it is a solid anchor in his life.

We may not always understand someone else's anchor points and may feel, "That wouldn't be an anchor point for me," but it doesn't have to be because it isn't yours! Yours is special only to you. Mine is special to me.

Diana Radabaugh tells an incredible story of an an-gelic visitation when she was less than a year old. Re-gardless of how you feel about angelic visitations, this has been an anchor point in her life that she has held onto and has never let go!

One of those anchor points is Bette Ramsey's book which God gave her, *"My Mother's Welcome Home,"* telling about her mother's entrance into heaven. This is something that you could not take out of Bette Ramsey with anything you might say or think. It is an anchor point in her life.

Check in your own life and see what God has given you that is your anchor point, and then thank Him for it every day, and hold onto it every day.

Chapter 12

When Reality Was Real

By Diana Radabaugh

God often gives us an unusual angelic experience for the particular moment and always for a specific purpose. However, angelic encounters can also be experienced many years before we understand the purpose for which the angel was sent.

Such is the case in the testimony, *"When Reality Was Real."*

Charles and Frances Hunter

This was the day, after all these days, months and years, when I would finally face the truth. Or would it be fiction? Dreams? Or was it a place of escape? As I bundled up my three children to take them out in the cold fall breeze, my mind was racing, my heart pounding with anticipation. Could I, would I, really have the guts to face this? After twenty-six years, how many times had I wondered if it really could have happened; a million times or more. Especially on beautiful spring days as I would look up at the blue skies with the different hues, as I would watch the dancing, fluffy, billowing, white clouds gently floating by. Could it have been? Who could I ask? Was it light beyond the darkness of the night? Is there density in clouds? As a child my mind so often wondered what the truth was.

Yet deep within my heart I always knew that my mother held the key to the truth. Somewhere within her memory she held the key. She was the one I had to go see. It was time. I won't even call, I'll just show up. If I call I might lose my courage.

As I put the children into the car to drive just the few miles to her home, suddenly I felt the steely determination to settle it once and for all. After all, I was twenty-six years old, how long would I go on thinking, "Did it really happen?" It seemed real, but things like this don't happen. I have never heard anyone else say that anything like this had happened to them. And if I had told anyone they would surely have thought I was crazy or they would have laughed at me. So many times I thought that, but no more. Today I am going to face the truth, whatever the truth is. I had to know, I just had to!

As I helped three-year-old Timmy off with his coat and told the children to go play in the toy room, I looked intensely at my mother. "Mom," I said, "I came here today to ask you a question ~ the most important question of my life. Please don't laugh at me or think I'm crazy, but I have to know something and you are the only one who has the answer." She sat down in her chair and, with timid hesitation, she said, "Okay, honey."

I found a piece of tablet paper, sat down at the kitchen table and started to draw a picture from my own memory, the memory of an infant, of one only a few months old. I had seen that picture thousands of times in my mind so it wasn't hard to draw. I just had to make sure it was just the way I remembered. A cozy little bedroom, just the right size for a baby. Against one wall was a dresser with a lamp that often burned a soft light bulb. To the left of the dresser was one of the windows. Against another wall was a short long dresser or toy box, on top of it rested a brown stuffed teddy bear and a couple of other stuffed animals. The third wall was the door, and there stood the baby bed. The light switch was over the bed just inside the door. The fourth wall had a window. Almost right in the middle of the room sat a high-back rocking chair with a soft blanket on the arm of the chair. Lying in front of the rocking chair was a colorful rag rug crocheted by my mother's mother. I gingerly picked up the piece of paper and walked over to where my mother sat looking completely mystified. I remember my hands were wet and my mouth was dry.

"Now, Mom, please think. Do you know where we lived when I was just a few months old, say seven or ten months old?" She looked up at me quite puzzled and said, "Why of course I do, Diana. Where you were first born." I continued, "Do you remember what my bedroom looked like? Do you remember anything about my room?"

"Well, for a couple of months you slept with me in my room since your dad was in the service. That was during World War II, but then, yes, you had your own little room. And, yes, I am sure I remember your room. Why?"

I thrust the piece of paper at her and said, "Oh, please, Mom! This is so important to me. Study this drawing and tell me if this is what my room looked like."

I was breathing very shallow as I intently waited for what seemed like hours for her reply, when in reality, it was only seconds.

She looked up at me with wonderment and said, "My God, Diana! You were only a few months old! How could you remember this?"

With a deep, deep sigh of overwhelming relief, I sat down in front of her on the footstool and began to tell her a story that I had held in for so long, a hidden secret, of when I used to fly.

One night while lying in my baby bed asleep, I heard a very persistent "Tap, tap, tap," on my window. "Tap, tap, tap!" Very annoyed at the sound, I looked above my head to where the sound was coming from. I looked and in the window, outlined by the darkness of the night, stood an angel. Communicating by thought rather than spoken words, the angel said, "Come unlock the window and come out." Communicating with thought also, I rather indignantly said, "I can't do that! Look, I'm only a baby!"

The angel said, "Yes, you can. Will yourself to, and you will be able to do it!"

I declined, knowing I just would not be able to do such a thing. It would be impossible! The angel gently yet firmly insisted that I could. I reluctantly agreed and instantly was there at the window trying to unlock it. Finally, through angelic instruction and the angel's help, I got the window open and off we flew. "Wow! This is great! Weightlessness!"

We flew until we flew past the darkness into the light, where the sky was so blue with different hues, where the clouds were so big, so fluffy, so white.

We flew right into the biggest billowing white cloud. I could hear the echoing of laughter; the excitement was so spectacular. No one had to tell me what to do, I just followed the giggles as if I had been there forever. I joined right in with all the activity. Received, welcomed and accepted as belonging, I entered with the others, playing and laughing. Oh, the freedom of joy!

This would happen night after night. My angel would come to my window and softly tap on the glass to alert me that it was time to go. I would be waiting. I could hardly wait until the beautiful angel would come to take me away to play in the clouds. I would go to the window (I never had to unlock the window or even open it after the first time ~ I don't know the "why's" of that, I just know it was so). We would fly fast, oh the freedom of weightlessness! It was exhilerating as we flew through the darkness toward the bright flashing stars into the brilliance of the day. We met there night after night. We, the "babies."

We met there to play with each other among the clouds. We would play "Train, who's the engine, who's the caboose, who are the cars?" We would crawl one after the other through the clouds then play tag, or we would bump headlong into each other and roll and tumble laughing and giggling.

The clouds were so beautiful! The density changed so that you could easily hide in the thickness. It was such fun to try to find each other as we played hide and seek. When we would play "trampoline," that was great ~ at the bottom of the cloud it was thick but the higher you jumped, the thinner the cloud became, and many at the same time would say, "Go!" and we would all jump high and play peek-a-boo, laughing and giggling. "I see you!" "No, I see you!" "Well, you can't see me!"

Someone would tickle your foot and off you would go, playing something else, jumping jacks, airplane. One we loved so much was stacking each other as high as we could, on one another's shoulders, laughing and giggling until we would hear through the moist clouds our particular name called out. Then we would cheerfully turn to the others and say, "I gotta go, see you later!"

The angels always enjoyed watching us play. I am sure we each enjoyed the glorious sight of seeing the many angels that stood around in little clusters just talking with each other. I remember looking at them, standing so regally and strong in their circle talking, sometimes seeming very serious. I would just wonder what they were talking about. But, oh well, I had to go back to something more important: PLAYING!

My angel was really stunningly beautiful, over the shoulder blonde wavy hair, with compelling, all-meaningful crystal blue eyes. A flowing glistening, shimmering white robe with an exquisite wide gold belt with a long rope that had tassles at the end. Barefoot!

At that time, I would call my angel by name but I

cannot recall what that name was. One night I heard my name echo through the clouds and immediately with warm cheeks flushed from the hard playing, I looked at my friends, my playmates, and with a big wave of my hand, said, "Bye! See ya' later!" I went to the side of my angel as the angel said goodnight to his companions.

We proceeded to fly and as I always did on our flights back, I would rattle off replaying some of the exciting events that took place as we played in the clouds. As we tumbled and laughed and sang, I was talking a hundred miles a minute, and then I realized that my angel was not at my side. I slowed down and looked back over my shoulder and my angel was far above me. I flew back to be at the angel's side and asked, "What's wrong?"

The angel said, "I have something to tell you. Tonight will be the last time you will fly. You must stay on earth now. The time has come for you to go!"

Without hesitation I said very firmly, "Oh, no. This cannot be the last time that I will fly! I have friends up there, they'll miss me, I have to go back!"

With no reserve, the angel said, "You cannot. Tonight will be the last time you will fly. You have a destiny to fulfill. You have a work that must be completed. But someday, I will see you on earth." Strongly I said, with my voice, "Well, you take me to Jesus!"

Now I never remember seeing Jesus or really ever even speaking about Him. It just seems like He was everything up there in the clouds, the color, the atmosphere, the laughter, the coolness of the clouds themselves, everything, even our breath.

I continued, "He will let me stay!" The angel said with authority, "No, He is the One who gave the order. You're getting too old. You must stay on earth now and complete your destiny."

With that, I was back in my baby bed crying and crying hard. Soon my mother was there picking me up in her arms, carrying me to the rocking chair where she tried to comfort me. But I would not be comforted.

Many years later, after I told my mother this story, I was with a Christian woman and felt a strong desire to share the story with her. I had only shared it with one other person in all those years, yet I felt a closeness with this lady and felt that she would enjoy hearing it.

The more I told her, the more frightened I became as the story unfolded. She appeared to become strangely quiet. When I finished, she looked at me through squinted eyes and said, "Why did that happen to you? You aren't any better than I am and it never happened to me!" I shuddered and said, "I don't know! I really don't know!"

As I drove home that night, my heart ached with rejection and pain. I cried out to the Lord, "God, why did You let me remember when I flew? She is right! She's as good as I am and she said it never happened to her. Why did it happen to me?" The night was silent and so was my God!

Several months later, alone in my home doing some little household tasks, the Lord clearly said to me as if I'd just asked Him the question of why I flew, "Oh, by the way, the reason I let you remember was because I wanted you to remember when reality was real. I would have lost you to darkness a long time ago had it not been for this memory."

I shuddered with the solemness of His statement. I thought back over my life! Raped by a male caretaker at the age of three, repeatedly raped by a female babysitter when I was eight, the oldest of six children with a brutal alcoholic father, seeing my mother often beaten, feeling the stings of hunger, cold and desolation, being molested by my dad, I married young to literally flee for my life. I thought back of running from one pain and rejection to another and having great marital problems and three children. Yes, I could understand a little bit more of His great wisdom in why He let me remember many times in many hard situations the times when I would tumble and turn, giggle and laugh as I would crawl through the clouds.

So many times in my life I would recall when I would fly with my angel. And it is true that the memory kept me sane and it gave me hope to remember that there was a place, a time when life was laughter, innocence and fun. A time when reality was real.

For He says to Moses, "I will have mercy on whomever I will have mercy, and I will have compassion on whomever I will have compassion" (Romans 9:15).

CHAPTER 13

My Mother's Welcome Home

There is a time to be born and a time to die!
(Ecclesiastes 3:2).

Death is inevitable and it comes to everyone!

Unless the rapture comes soon, many living today will experience death.

When we think of someone dying, many thoughts come racing into our minds. We immediately visualize the person who has departed from this life in a casket and then the next picture will be the casket being lowered into the ground with many tears being shed over the sad event!

We should never think of a person and how they would look in a casket because the moment our bodies take their last breath, the very split second our hearts beat for the last time in this shell where it has lived for a certain number of years, "we" are no longer in that body because when the earthly signal for death has come, our soul and spirit have departed and we are in heaven to spend eternity with God and Jesus! The angels are present to escort us!

When we think about exiting from this life in that fashion, it will take away many of the tears which we might shed. The Life Application Bible explains death in a footnote in a most beautiful, unusual way. It says,

> *"For many, death is a darkened door at the end of their lives, a passageway to an unknown and feared destiny. But for God's people, death is a bright doorway to a new and better life. So why do we fear death? Is it because of the pain we expect, the separation from loved ones, the surprise of it? God can help us deal with those fears. He has shown us that death is just another step in the continuing eternal life we began when we started to follow him. Death is not final; it is the first step into eternity."*

When Bette Ramsey's mother died, God gave her a vision that He directed her to write which can change your thinking about the horrible thing many perceive death to be. As you read Bette Ramsey's story of "My Mother's Welcome Home," think about this the next time a friend or family member passes into eternity.

Charles and Frances Hunter

My Mother's Welcome Home
by Bette Ramsey

This story is a memorial to my mother who went to live with Jesus on December 30, 1975 at 9:15 PM.

In the midst of my deepest heartaches, the good Lord gave me the words I write in this book. He dried the tears and took away the pain. He calmed my nerves and comforted my heart.

Long before time to put the sun out, the Master of the Guard for Heaven's Pearly Gates had started another day. The first thing on his agenda was to check the calendar for the most important events of the day.

Already it was December 30, 1975. Oh, what a busy time. Today preparations must be made to receive one of the Lord's faithful servants. He had a host of people to see before mid-morning.

Briefcase in hand, the Master of the Guard hurried to the Celestial Room where Gabriel, Heaven's Maitre d' and a host of biblical saints would soon assemble.

On the way, he stopped off at the choir room. There he briefly discussed with the choir director some of the music required for the evening events.

The choir was already in rehearsal. The music filled his heart anew with praises unto the Lord Jesus Christ. What a beautiful welcome this child of the King would receive, thought the Master of the Guard as he hurried on his way.

"But the saints of the Most High shall receive

*the kingdom, and possess the kingdom forever,
even forever and ever'"* (Daniel 7:18).

The Master of the Guard was first to arrive. While
he waited for the others, he had time to take a quick
glance into the Christian biography of tonight's new
resident.

It read: Lela Francis McQuatters Ramsey. Sins
washed away by the blood of the Jesus Christ, February,
1941.

*And the ransomed of the Lord shall return, And
come to Zion with singing, With everlasting joy
on their heads. They shall obtain joy and gladness, And sorrow and sighing shall flee away*
(Isaiah 35:10).

*Blessed are those who do His commandments,
that they may have the right to the tree of life,
and may enter through the gates into the city* (Revelation 22:14).

...Interrupted by the appearance of Gabriel, The
Master of the Guard looked up and smiled.

*And the construction of its wall was of jasper; and
the city was pure gold, like clear glass* (Rev. 21:18).

"Gabriel," he said, "what a blessed time this is for
us. We are privileged to welcome another dear saint
home to heaven."

"Yes, I know," Gabriel replied. "I've just come from

the Throne Room. Jesus told me. Tonight I lead the trumpets in the Welcome Home March for Lela Ramsey. And from what I perceive about her, it will be my pleasure to be able to welcome her home."

Before Gabriel could finish his last sentence, Heaven's Maitre d' came into the room and listened. He couldn't help but think of words to finish Gabriel's sentence. "...where there'll be no more worries, no more heartaches, no more tears. For Jesus washes them all away."

After greeting everyone all around, the Master of the Guard asked, "Are you making ready for tonight's welcome dinner?"

"Yes, I stopped by the banquet hall on my way from the kitchen. Everything's going according to schedule."

By this time saints were arriving in twos and threes. While they steadily filed into the Celestial Conference Room, the Master of the Guard held Gabriel's attention. "I must see Jesus about the family that's left behind, and their care." He said speaking his thoughts aloud:

Behold, I tell you a mystery: We shall not all sleep, but we shall all be changed ~ in a moment, in the twinkling of an eye, at the last trumpet. For the trumpet will sound, and the dead will be raised incorruptible, and we shall be changed. For this corruptible must put on incorruption, and this mortal must put on immortality (I Corinthians 15:51-53).

Gabriel was pleased to answer, "Jesus has taken care of that. An Angel of Mercy will be with each one, to comfort and guide them. Even tho this family is serving the Master, none of them will willingly give up their Mother. They don't understand, really. They fear the unknown; but God is a merciful God, so each will have a renewed strength from the Holy Spirit. Too, her husband and children know God's holy word, and will find comfort in the scriptures."

Comfort is based on knowledge. *Know* appears in the Bible seven hundred and fifty-three times. For instance, in II Corinthians 5:1,

> *For we know that if our earthly house, this tent, is destroyed, we have a building from God, a house not made with hands, eternal in the heavens.*

The Master of the Guard nodded his head; he approved of every word Gabriel had said.

"I think the Angels of Comfort will refer to Hebrews 11:16,

> *But now they desire a better, that is, a heavenly country. Therefore God is not ashamed to be called their God, for He has prepared a city for them.*

Gabriel agreed. He added, "I know one will surely quote Psalms 116:15,

> *Precious in the sight of the Lord is the death of His saints.*

> *"He who has an ear, let him hear what the Spirit*

says to the churches. To him who overcomes I will give to eat from the tree of life, which is in the midst of the Paradise of God"(Revelation 2:7).

The Maitre d' had held his silence long enough. He wanted to add a word of wisdom, too.

"From what I've seen of this family, I'm sure the children will long remember things their mother taught them. As in Proverbs 31:1,

The words of King Lemuel, the utterance which his mother taught him.

The Master of the Guard nodded his head in agreement. Jesus loved the people of the world so much that he gave up his heavenly home and went to earth to be born of the Virgin Mary. To the world, he grew up as a son of a common carpenter. Yet, as a child, he confounded the intellects with his knowledge. And as he grew older, Christ performed miracles, healed the sick, raised the dead and died on the cross of Calvary. He paid the price so that the world might have life eternal. And now one of the believers was joining him in Glory this night!

The Master of the Guard stood up. "We can stay around here and talk about the goodness of God all day. But I must get on with the day's preparations. So if you'll excuse me, I'll get started with the business of the traditional reception line... It looks as though we have more than enough to make our new resident welcome."

"*And I give them eternal life, and they shall never*

perish; neither shall anyone snatch them out of My hand" (John 10:28).

Her mother and sister were there, accompanied by several of her friends. All were anxious for her arrival. They already knew that she had had her last heartache. There would be no more sorrow, from now on she would live and reign with the Master forever!

It seems impossible for so many to gather willingly to form a reception line to welcome just one soul to heaven. When the Master of the Guard looked again and saw all of the saints gathered there, he began to pick out different ones and silently reflected upon them. He saw Deborah, the prophetess, talking to Mary, the mother of Jesus, and Ruth, Esther, and Naomi. How proper for her to be present. She was a woman of unfaltering faith in God, like Abraham, who stood a few feet away, surrounded by David, Joshua and Moses.

Then there was Jacob speaking in low tones to another group. He once spent a night wrestling with an angel of the Lord, and would not let the angel go until the angel blessed him. His life was an assurance that God would not turn away from those who repented.

"He who believes in the Son has everlasting life; and he who does not believe the Son shall not see life, but the wrath of God abides on him." (John 3:36).

In that same group sat Joseph taking in every word. His brothers sold him to a band of Ishamelites on their way to Egypt. Rather then become bitter and full of hatred, he turned his heart and thoughts to God. Even when he was tested with fiery trials, Joseph was true to God. His high principles triumphed.

Noah and another group could be seen further back. He had stood like a rock when surrounded by contempt and ridicule. Amid the prevailing corruption of the world, Noah had labored under the explicit guidance of the true God.

In the midst of all of these and many, many more Old Testament saints, some of the New Testament men and women were present. A quick glance showed Peter, Paul, James and John; then there were Lazarus and his sisters, Mary and Martha, and so many more.

Time was growing short. The Master of the Guard called the assembly to attention and quickly directed each in his responsibility.

It was late by the time he had finished with all of the preparations of receiving a new resident. Each one hurried away to prepare for the great occasion.

For there is no partiality with God. (Rom. 2:11).

About a quarter until nine, Jesus walked out onto the balcony, leaned over and watched the Heavenly carriage drawn by six white thoroughbreds gallop down the streets of gold.

The horses were harnessed in diamond-studded halters. The sparkle emitted from the gems on the harness radiated a great sprinkling of glitter. So great was the brightness that the natural man could not behold it.

The angels assigned to comfort the family led the great procession, closely followed by the soldiers acting as Royal Guards for the coach and its precious cargo. The coachman drove the six white horses at a lively pace. He knew the exact instant to arrive.

As they made their way down the streets of gold, the footman looked around and saw the beauty of it all. On either side were fountains of pure water flowing from springs of living water. In the sky above, doves and other birds of the air sailed, forming their own acknowledgment of the hour. While out in the fields of green, the calf and the lion rested underneath a sprawling bush. For it is written,

> *"The wolf also shall dwell with the lamb, the leopard shall lie down with the young goat, the calf and the young lion and the fatling together; and a little child shall lead them. The cow and the bear shall graze; their young ones shall lie down together; And the lion shall eat straw like the ox. The nursing child shall play by the cobra's hole, and the weaned child shall put his hand in the viper's den. They shall not hurt nor destroy in all My holy mountain, for the earth shall be full of the knowledge of the Lord as the waters cover the sea"* (Isaiah 11:6-9).

The caravan proceeded, passing a garden whose artistry was incomparable to its beauty. Its surface was variegated with hills and plains, interspersed with lovely brooks and lakes. The shapely shrubs edged delicate flowers and the heights of the hills were adorned with trees in pure, clean air.

The groves of trees in Heaven's orchards were laden with delicious fruits of every variety. Their branches drooped under the heavy load of tempting fruit of the sweetest and most fragrant kind.

The vast plains were dressed with an unlimited wealth of beauty, while the buildings were furnished in gold, silver, jasper and gems of every precious stone. All this existed in abundance.

As the Angelic Caravan passed by the beauty that decorated Heaven's landscape, they glanced around with delight and rejoiced again at the wonders of God's creation.

And this is the promise that He has promised us ~ eternal life (I John 2:25).

For he who sows to his flesh will of the flesh reap corruption, but he who sows to the Spirit will of the Spirit reap everlasting life (Gal. 6:8).

They passed Abraham, Isaac and Jacob, then David, John, Paul and Peter and a host of others hurrying to the banquet room to form the reception line to welcome the new resident.

Everything was on schedule. The Lord had everything in control. Jesus walked back into the throne room where Gabriel waited his instructions.

It was 9:15 p.m.

The Lord signaled Gabriel.

Far away Lela heard the trumpet as Gabriel began to play taps. She said to the family, "I'm going now." And with those words gave herself into the Lord's hands.

The coach had pulled up in front of the little old house on the wrong side of the tracks. While the Heavenly Footman jumped down and rolled out a plush velvet red carpet sprinkled with pure gold dust, Lela accompanied the angel the Lord had sent to escort her to his side. Then the Footman swung open the coach door and the Coachman assisted her to a comfortable seat made of velvet, trimmed in pure silk. Lela relaxed in a haven of luxury, and off they raced up into the heavens where Jesus waited to receive his own.

While the Heavenly Coach and its escort spiraled from earth to heaven, Jesus went into the Crown Room.

But now having been set free from sin, and having become slaves of God, you have your fruit to holiness, and the end, everlasting life (Romans 6:22).

After much consideration he picked out a crown heavy with diamonds, rubies, sapphires, opals and gems of every heavenly description.

This finished, Jesus left the Palace and made his way to the Pearly Gates where he would welcome his own.

The entourage pulled up in front of the Pearly Gates about the same time Jesus arrived. The Master of the Guard of the Pearly Gates unlocked the gates. As they swung open, Jesus stepped forward and exclaimed, "Welcome home my good and faithful servant, enter into the joys of my land."

Lela fell to her knees and worshiped her Savior! There

were so many things for which she wanted to thank and praise Him.

Jesus stretched forth His hand and said, "Come, my child, you have been faithful over a few things, now I will make you ruler over many things."

The Lord joined Lela in the coach and off they sped to the palace. He accompanied her to the Throne Room where she was clothed in white raiment and crowned with the crown of righteousness.

Now it was time. Jesus escorted Lela to the Banquet Room. Here the music rang out loud and clear.

Blessed is the man who endures temptation; for when he has been proved, he will receive the crown of life which the Lord has promised to those who love Him (James 1:12).

She heard the harps of gold, following the sounding of the trumpets as they hailed a welcome.

The Heavenly Doorman opened the Banquet Room door. And Jesus said, "For you my child, all this to welcome you home!"

Lela stood awed. When she finally could speak she said, "Now I truly understand I Corinthians 2:9,

But as it is written, "Eye has not seen, nor ear heard, nor have entered into the heart of man the things which God has prepared for those who love Him."

The Angelic Choir, ten thousand in number, sang while the Heavenly orchestra played. Together Jesus and

Lela walked into the Banquet Room where her mother and sister and brother, along with a host of other saints, stood in the reception line waiting to welcome my Mother home.

For the Lord God is a sun and shield; the Lord will give grace and glory; no good thing will He with-hold from those who walk uprightly (Psalm 84:11).

His angels are active while we live on earth, but Jesus gives us a peek into eternity where we will live in the future, and what angels will be doing to welcome us into heaven!

Revelation
The New Jerusalem

Then I saw a new heaven and a new earth, for the old heaven and the old earth had disappeared. And the sea was also gone. And I saw the holy city, the new Jerusalem, coming down from God out of heaven like a beautiful bride prepared for her husband.

I heard a loud shout from the throne saying, "Look, the home of God is now among his people! He will live with them, and they will be his people. God himself with be with them. He will remove all of their sorrows, and there will be no more death or sorrow or crying or pain. For the old world and its evils are gone forever."

And the one sitting on the throne said, "Look, I am making all things new!" And then he said to me, "Write this down, for what I tell you is trustworthy and true." And he also said, "It is finished! I am the Alpha and the Omega - the Beginning and the End. To all who are thirsty I will give the springs of the water of life without charge! All who are victorious will inherit all these blessings, and I will be their God, and they will be my children. But cowards who turn away from me, and unbelievers, and the corrupt, and murderers, and the immoral, and those who practice witchcraft, and idol worshipers, and all liars - their doom is in the lake that burns with fire and sulphur. This is the second death."

Then one of the seven angels who held the seven bowls containing the seven last plagues came and said to me, "Come with me! I will show you the bride, the wife of the Lamb."

So he took me in spirit to a great, high mountain, and he showed me the holy city, Jerusalem, descending out of heaven from God. It was filled with the glory of God and sparkled like a precious gem, crystal clear like jasper. Its walls were broad and high, with twelve gates guarded by twelve angels. And the names of the twelve tribes of Israel were written on the gates. There were three gates on each side-east, north, south, and west. The wall of the city had twelve foundation stones, and on them were written the names of the twelve apostles of the Lamb.

The angel who talked to me held in his hand a gold measuring stick to measure the city, its gates, and its walls. When he measured it, he found it was a square, as wide as it was long. In fact, it was in the form of a cube, for its length and width and height were each 1,400 miles. Then he measured the walls and found them to be 216 feet thick (the angel used a standard human measure).

The wall was made of jasper, and the city was pure gold,

as clear as glass. The wall of the city was built on foundation stones inlaid with twelve gems: the first was jasper, the second sapphire, the third agate, the fourth emerald, the fifth onyx, the sixth carnelian, the seventh chrysolite, the eighth beryl, the ninth topaz, the tenth chrysoprase, the eleventh jacinth, the twelfth amethyst.

The twelve gates were made of pearls — each gate from a single pearl! And the main street was pure gold, as clear as glass.

No temple could be seen in the city, for the Lord God Almighty and the Lamb are its temple. And the city has no need of sun or moon, for the glory of God illuminates the city, and the Lamb is its light. The nations of the earth will walk in its light, and the rulers of the world will come and bring their glory to it. Its gates never close at the end of day because there is no night. And all the nations will bring their glory and honor into the city. Nothing evil will be allowed to enter—no one who practices shameful idolatry and dishonesty — but only those whose names are written in the Lamb's Book of Life.

And the angel showed me a pure river with the water of life, clear as crystal, flowing from the throne of God and of the Lamb, coursing down the center of the main street. On each side of the river grew a tree of life, bearing twelve crops of fruit, with a fresh crop each month. The leaves were used for medicine to heal the nations.

No longer will anything be cursed. For the throne of God and of the Lamb will be there, and his servants will worship him. And they will see his face, and his name will be written on their foreheads. And there will be no night there—no need for lamps or sun — for the Lord God will shine on them. And they will reign forever and ever.

Then the angel said to me, "These words are trustworthy and true: 'The Lord God, who tells his prophets what the future holds, has sent his angel to tell you what will happen soon.'"

Jesus is Coming

"Look, I am coming soon! Blessed are those who obey the prophecy written in this scroll."

I, John, am the one who saw and heard all these things. And when I saw and heard these things, I fell down to worship the angel who showed them to me. But again he said, "No, don't worship me. I am a servant of God, just like you and your brothers the prophets, as well as all who obey what is written in the scroll. Worship God!"

Then he instructed me, "Do not seal up the prophetic words you have written, for the time is near. Let the one who is doing wrong continue to do wrong; the one who is vile, continue to be vile; the one who is good, continue to do good; and the one who is holy, continue in holiness."

"See, I am coming soon, and my reward is with me, to repay all according to their deeds. I am the Alpha and the Omega, the First and the Last, the Beginning and the End."

Blessed are those who wash their robes so they can enter through the gates of the city and eat the fruit from the tree of life. Outside the city are the dogs - the sorcerers, the sexually immoral, the murderers, the idol worshipers, and all who love to live a lie.

"I, Jesus, have sent my angel to give you this message for the churches. I am both the source of David and the heir to his throne. I am the bright morning star."

The Spirit and the bride say, "Come." Let each one who hears them say, "Come." Let the thirsty ones come - anyone who wants to. Let them come and drink the water of life without charge. And I solemnly declare to everyone who hears the prophetic words of this book: If anyone adds anything to what is written here, God will add to that person the plagues described in this book. And if anyone removes any of the words of this prophetic book, God will remove that person's share in the tree of life and in the holy city that are described in this book.

He who is the faithful witness to all these things says, "Yes, I am coming soon!"

Amen! Come, Lord Jesus!

The grace of the Lord Jesus be with you all.

(Revelation 21, 22 NLT)

How to Heal the Sick
Charles and Frances Hunter

A loved one is sick…your friend was just in an accident…a family member is facing an emotional crisis. At times our hearts ache with the desire to help, but either we don't know how or we are afraid and stop short. The truth is that, as a Christian, the Holy Spirit within you is ready to heal the sick! Charles and Frances Hunter present solid, biblically based methods of healing that can bring not only physical health, but also spiritual wholeness and the abundant life to you, your family, and everyone around you.

ISBN: 978-0-88368-600-3 • Trade • 224 pages

Handbook for Healing (revised)
Charles and Frances Hunter

In this recently updated and expanded edition, Charles and Frances Hunter present the keys to healing that they have found in the Bible and through the innovations of medical science. Written as a complement to the their best-selling *How to Heal the Sick,* this book is essential for your library—and your ministry. Discover that God can use you to bring healing and help to family, friends, and everyone you come in contact with. No longer will you have to stand by, helpless, when people are hurting!

ISBN: 978-0-88368-705-5 • Trade • 224 pages

---

www.whitakerhouse.com